COUNTERSTRIKE & OTHER MUSINGS

DAVID STRIKE

Flat Island Publishing

Copyright © 2022 by David Strike

All rights reserved. No part of this publication may be reproduced, distributed or transmitted in any form or by any means, including photocopying, recording, or other electronic or mechanical methods, without the prior written permission of the publisher, except in the case of brief quotations embodied in critical reviews and certain other non-commercial uses permitted by copyright law.

Flat Island Publishing, Hong Kong

Book Layout ©2022 Flat Island Publishing

Cover Image by Roy Bisson Cartoons & Design, PO Box 5 Wickham, NSW 2293, Australia, roybisso@optusnet.com.au

Counterstrike & Other Musings/David Strike. 1st ed.

ISBN-13: 979-8409644369

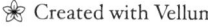 Created with Vellum

CONTENTS

Forewarned ... 7

COUNTERSTRIKE
1. The Beagle has stranded. ... 13
2. There's a plaice for us ... 16
3. Sex and thugs and male control ... 20
4. Fee, Phy, Ho, Hum ... 23
5. A picture's worth a thousand nerds ... 26
6. Pardon me, myth, my narcosis is showing ... 29
7. Here there be monsters – and bugs ... 32
8. Just when you thought it was safe ... 35
9. All A-bored ... 38
10. Minding your P's in Q's ... 42
11. Tanks for the memories ... 45
12. An image worth framing ... 48
13. The little shop of horrors ... 52
14. I did it my weigh ... 55
15. Writing a wrong ... 58
16. Sum fizzy-ology ... 61
17. Trash or treasure ... 64
18. What a guy ... 67
19. Ve haf vays of making you tock ... 71
20. Think or thwim ... 75
21. Whither goest thou? ... 78
22. No fear! ... 81
23. Heroes and villains ... 84
24. Laying down the law ... 87
25. Getting the third degree ... 91
26. A chain reaction ... 95
27. Talk's cheap. Technology isn't ... 99
28. I wish I'd said that ... 103

29. Heads and tales	107
30. Fit for nothing	111
31. The diver's prayer	114
32. To 'air' is human ...???	118
33. How To survive a dive show	122
34. Deep thoughts	127
35. Biting the hand that feeds you	131
36. The cold war	135
37. Survival of the fittest	139
38. Hear today. Gone tomorrow	143
39. At the going down of the sun ...	147
40. Shape up or ship out	151
41. The gee! spot	155
42. The evil aye	159
43. Colour me blue	163
44. Stamp out coccolithophores – and penguins	167
45. Stuff and nonsense	170
46. Manual dexterity	173
47. A lesson in lunacy	177
48. Mocha do about nothing	181
49. The wongs of a dive	185
50. Firkin about	188
51. A funny thing happened on the way to the forum	191
52. The things we do for love	195
53. In love with life	199
54. Turn your head and cough	203
55. Gone fission	207
56. Pot luck	210

ZYMURGY INC.

57. Uranus – the world's first Nitrox snorkel	217
58. The Polly-Gaff gas analyser	219
59. The Mollusc Fu-2	222
60. Missile Fins	225
61. Weigh-2-Go	228
62. Titanic II: A rebreather breakthrough	230

"When I were down an 'undred feet or more ... "

FOREWARNED

I am not sure anymore what on solid earth compelled me to start a diving magazine back in 1992. But I remember having visions of long gratis diving holidays, interspersed by short sorties to the office to pick up money. That was prior to the first bills hitting home, of course.

At the time, I knew even less about publishing than about diving, and promptly came face to face with the harsh realities of the media business. One is that the only way you can make a small fortune in publishing is by starting off with a big one. The other is that you are lost between the white sheets unless you find first-rate people to help you.

Thanks to Julia Goh, our superb Editor, who later joined me in my subsequent media ventures, we did in the end manage to print the first two issues of Asian Diver. What was acutely missing though was any hint of income. And with cashflow in full reverse, I decided to do the right thing and started looking for advertising sales representatives.

After all, it's money that makes the printing press go round.

Armed with a surplus of enthusiasm and unhindered by any common sense, I wrote to about 30 'Media Reps' around the world, explaining in full colour the superb business opportunity I was presenting to them. Sell ads for Asian Diver and dive into a mountain of easy cash. That sort of thing.

The learning curve was steep. After several weeks and with our cashflow turning a bloody red, nobody had responded. Things went from bad to desperate.

Until the call from Sydney came.

I had gone out for a liquid lunch that day to drown my sorrows. When I got back to the office, a troubled looking Julia told me of an odd phone call she had received from a certain "David Strike" from some Australian media company. Apparently, he had told her in no uncertain terms that he would commit ritual suicide on national TV if we were to refuse to appoint him as our sales agent for all Pacific Islands – including those that didn't exist yet. And for Australia, of course.

A ray of hope. Finally.

Despite Julia's suggestion to dispatch David to a counsellor rather than doing business with him, I called him immediately and told him that after thorough deliberation, I had decided to put him on. My reasoning was simple – if someone was zany enough to want to do business with us, who were we to send him to a shrink. If anything, that was where I belonged for starting such a magazine in the first place.

The rest, as they say, is hysterical.

In no time, "Strikey" became my close friend, dive buddy,

occasional shrink and BBQ instructor. Asian Diver found in him a trusted writer and tireless sales person. His inimitable sense of humour, his ability to always strike the right chord with people and his cosmic talent for storytelling helped us through the rough spots and are an integral part of the success Asian Diver became over time.

The book you are holding in your hand now is a treasure chest of his insights, his wisdom and his vast knowledge ... even if he tries so very hard all the time to coat it with self-deprecating humour.

In doing so, he reveals who he truly is: One of a kind.

Rainer Sigel
Founder, Asian Diver Magazine

COUNTERSTRIKE

In 1995, Rainer Sigel – founder and Publisher of Asia's first diving publication – invited me to write a regular column for inclusion in his magazine. The brief that he gave me was, to say the least, 'flexible': I could write about any diving topic that took my fancy ... providing that it didn't entail his appearance in court to defend a libel suit.

Fortunately for our continuing friendship, nothing that I subsequently wrote warranted the attention of a lawyer. Nor – and probably to my better credit as far as Rainer was concerned - did it appear to trigger a stampede of advertisers heading out of the door. Nevertheless, the whimsically titled *'CounterStrike'* column still allowed me a wonderful opportunity to lampoon an activity that sometimes takes itself too seriously: and all too often – especially where safety is concerned – not seriously enough.

Able to draw on nearly six decades spent in a variety of diving roles, my personal misadventures and occasional lapses in good judgement provided more than enough material for a regular magazine column; one that still continues to appear in a number of regional diving publications.

With an irreverent take on sometimes-serious diving issues – ranging from training and practical diving techniques, through to marine conservation, equipment and safety – it is easier to introduce this book by telling the reader what it is **NOT** about.

Although it contains elements of diving's past, it's not a history book. Nor is it about: underwater photography, technical diving, health & fitness, physics, philosophy, equipment, training programmes, dive travel, marine life, the environment, political correctness, or any of the other topics covered in its pages. Neither is it intended to be critical of divers who, having given considerable thought to their own practices, advance our better knowledge of diving.

It is, in fact, nothing more than a collection of light-hearted commentaries peopled with largely fictitious characters. However, should the reader discover a little of themselves in the following pages then it may well be time to give serious thought to those diving manuals gathering dust on their bookshelves.

And that's one of the great paradoxes of diving: That those who get the most fun and enjoyment out of the activity are usually those people who take it the most seriously.

David Strike

CHAPTER 1
THE BEAGLE HAS STRANDED.

Without doubt one of the best-remembered events of the last century will be that moment, in July 1969, when Neil Armstrong announced to a waiting audience back on Earth, *"The Eagle has landed"*. Climbing down from the lunar landing module onto the surface of the moon, his triumphant phrase, *"That's one small step for man, one giant leap for mankind!"* captured the world's imagination. It was a remarkable testament to human ingenuity and courage: A feat that, we believed, would pave the way for the exploration of worlds beyond our own.

In 1943, an equally significant – but less well-publicised – event took place in the Marne River, outside Paris. Lacking Armstrong's stirring oratory, Emile Gagnan, co-designer of the Aqualung, simply cried out, *"Mon Dieu, Jacques! I thought you had drowned!"* (The person in question hadn't! And Jacques Cousteau, went on to become one of the most famed underwater explorers of our time.)

It's now more than sixty years since the pair perfected their SCUBA diving regulator; a device that heralded new opportunities in mankind's attempts to freely explore the seventy-one per-cent of our planet that's hidden by water. But despite diving's growing popularity we've progressed very little in our exploration of 'inner space'! While we've been busy splashing around at the ocean's edge, mankind's attention has still remained focussed on the stars.

In some respects, sitting on top of a launch rocket waiting for somebody to push a button and send you hurtling off into outer space is a breeze when compared with diving. While engineers and physicists have mastered the technical difficulties of sending men on a 384,000 km journey to the moon, (and even sorted out the logistical problems of what fillings to put in the crew's lunchbox sandwiches, and how much clean underwear they'll require for a 33,000,000 kilometre voyage to Mars) none of them have fathomed out ways to put even an exceptionally well equipped diver to depths much beyond 300-metres.

But imagine what diving might have achieved had Cousteau and Gagnan's pioneering effort received the attention and support of unlimited government funding? Or had, in 1959, somebody of the stature of a President Kennedy, broadcast to the world:

"We choose to go to the sea-floor, not because it is easy, but because it is hard."?---

"This is the, '*S.S. Grumpy Grouper*', to Mission Control. Divers Sprat and Mackerel have entered the water and are initiating descent - now!"

"Roger that, '*Grumpy Grouper*'. This is Mission Control to divers, Sprat and Mackerel. How do you copy?"

"Brrlluubb! We read you just fine, Mission Control. We're now passing the 5-metre mark. 8-metres! ..."

"Mission Control here. You're looking good, Sprat!"

" ... 10-metres ... 12-metres. Touch down! Mission Control, we have touch-down."

"Mission Control to Sprat and Mackerel. Well done, guys! All instrument readings show normal. Continue with your planned dive."

"Brrlluubb! This is Sprat to Mission Control: I'm having difficulty keeping up with Mackerel. He's just chased a parrot-fish around a coral outcrop. It was one small fin-kick for him, but it's a giant swim for me. Brrlluubb! I can't see him! I've lost contact, Mission Control. I've lost him!"

"Mission Control to Sprat. Stay calm! Remember your Standard Operating Procedure: A quick search for no longer than one-minute and then surface. Do you copy that, *'Grumpy Grouper'*?"

"This is *'Grumpy Grouper'* to Mission Control. Both divers have surfaced two-metres from a nearby sand bank. Diver recovery vessel, *'Bubbly Beagle'*, is launched and on its way. Oh, Oh, *'Bubbly Beagle'* appears to have grounded in the shallows! Do you copy that, Mission Control? The *'Beagle'* has stranded!"

"Mission Control, here. That's not going to sound good in the history books. I knew I shouldn't have used Sprat to catch Mackerel!"

It took vision, commitment and money to get man to the moon. Just think what – given that same level of support – diving might be capable of accomplishing in the new millennium!

CHAPTER 2
THERE'S A PLAICE FOR US

I know that it's probably something that all marine biologists learn to do very early on in their career, but at a personal level I've never been able to tell the difference between a good looking fish and an ugly one within the same species.

And on that subject, I may as well confess that as far as most marine-life is concerned, I have just as much difficulty in telling a boy-critter from a girl-critter.

Not that it's always a clear-cut issue. Take those colourful slug-like creatures called nudibranchs: They're hermaphrodites with the sexual functions of both male and female. Although they've probably been given every opportunity to better themselves they still don't know whether they're Arthur or Martha! They mate as males, adopt the female role to lay eggs and then they die.

Some fish species, like groupers, are equally as versatile where gender is concerned. As soon as the male in a group dies the dominant female in the harem undergoes a complete sex change.

It's the sort of bizarre behaviour that's prompted a friend of mine, John Nitrox, to begin compiling a book that's already been described as, *"Doing for coral reefs what 'Melrose Place' did for the suburbs: Makes you wonder about the neighbours"*, a work-in-progress that's already being overshadowed by the efforts of another scientist who's recently published a paper suggesting that attractive male fish die young.

After spending an entire year observing female fish and seeing which males of the species they spend the most time with, the marine biologist – whose findings recently appeared in an internationally respected scientific journal – has concluded that sexy males die young, apparently worn out by the attentions of females of their kind who want to ensure good looking offspring.

On the other hand this researcher also reasons that the ugly ones live longer and actually have more opportunities to mate.

Leaving to one side the fact that sticking rigidly to either a masculine or feminine role isn't a high priority as far as some sea-life's concerned, I'm not altogether convinced that fish place too much emphasis on superficial things like appearance.

Take bottom-dwelling flatfish like plaice and halibut. They start out in life as perfectly symmetrical, good-looking guys with regular habits until, after a month or so of swimming around enjoying themselves in the ocean, they begin a metamorphosis.

The left eye begins to migrate over the top of the head where it ends up on the right side of the body in a process that twists the skull. The small fish then drops to the floor of the sea and begins its adult existence permanently lying on its left side gazing wistfully upwards from the sand.

Being underwater seems to encourage strange and peculiar changes of this sort; a transformation in which seemingly normal creatures can sometimes turn into very unattractive specimens.

"Excuse me! I don't have anyone to dive with and wondered whether I could buddy up with you?"

"Done much diving?"

"'fraid not. I only completed my entry-level diving course last week."

"That's obvious by the fact that you're wearing a snorkel. Real divers never bother with a snorkel! You're going to have to make some changes if you want to dive with me, and you can start by forgetting all of that rubbish that your instructor taught you: Especially the stuff about depth limits and such like.

"Anyone that I dive with has to prove that they're capable of diving down to 60-metres by themselves and picking up a handful of sand from the sea-bed. If they can't do that then they'll never be a good diver. And don't believe all of that nonsense that you've been told about the effects of nitrogen on the human body. I regularly dive to 70-plus metres on air and I've never felt anything other than good.

"As for the buddy system ... that's nothing but a load of twaddle! If you can't ... Oooh! Ow! Just a slight twinge – nothing to worry about, I'll just lay down on my left side for an hour or two and it'll soon pass.

"Tell you what! Why don't you go and spend the next month or so swimming around some shallow reefs and when you come back, I'll start showing you what real diving's all about?"

Despite what the marine biologist claims, it's difficult to imagine ugliness of that sort enjoying a long life beneath the sea!

CHAPTER 3
SEX AND THUGS AND MALE CONTROL

"Barely fifty-years old yet recreational diving is - in cultural terms - still in the Dark Ages: An activity dominated by male thugs with rampant hormones." Says Professor Greta Wrassebender, author of the internationally acclaimed, *"The Ultimate Aphrodisiac: A study of sexuality and cold, wet neoprene."*

And yet, when it comes to diving, sexual equality has never been an issue. Women win, hands down. Proven to have greater mental and physical endurance than men, women can withstand lower temperatures; are less likely to take unnecessary risks; have a greater tendency to support team efforts, and are generally more considerate of their buddy's needs.

Despite these genetic advantages the fact remains that diving, as a co-operative effort rather than a competitive activity, is still falling short in its efforts to attract more women.

Although the annual growth rate in the numbers of women learning to dive is steadily increasing, (variously reported as now being between 30 - 40% of the total numbers of entry-level students), the retention rates are still low: Few women - less than 10% - even bothering to try and break through the 'bubble-barrier', (diving's equivalent of the 'glass ceiling'!), to become Instructors or Instructor Trainers.

According to Professor Wrassebender, the problem is one of attitude. Based on a cherished belief buried deep in the male psyche that diving is a test of courage and proof of manhood, some insecure souls regard women who dive as a challenge to their masculinity.

"In the natural world the male of the species often exhibits gaudier markings or plumage than does the female." She says. "The more flamboyant the external appearance the greater the chances of attracting a suitable mate and ensuring survival of the species. For some men the dubious status associated with being a diving instructor is the diving equivalent of a peacock's tail feathers; imagined proof that they are sexually irresistible.

"This situation is often exacerbated by those women who, when learning to dive, unconsciously adopt a stereotyped role." Maintains Professor Wrassebender. "Conditioned by centuries of social pressure many women, apprehensive when confronted by a new learning experience such as diving, fall back on role-playing, regarding themselves as the *nurturer/follower* and the male as the *hunter/leader; p*ositions that encourage sexual discrimination that, in its most extreme form, may manifest itself as sexual harassment."

Studies among female divers of different levels of training and experience revealed that sexual harassment, although relatively uncommon, was most likely to occur at the entry level phase of diver training when the student diver was, through lack of knowledge, at her most vulnerable. The incidents range from unnecessary physical contact by an Instructor or divemaster, through to indecent proposals.

In a few instances the harassment was alleged to be perceived rather than real! Instructors subsequently claiming that the 'physical contact' was nothing more than holding a student's hand in an attempt to re-assure them during the early, open water phase of training, or a fumbled attempt to check the fit of a wet suit by means of the pinch and squeeze test, and that comments intended to be flirtatious ("'Ello, Darlin'! How about it, then?"), had been mis-interpreted!

Perhaps because of their strength of character - not to mention their acquired ability to deliver a stinging witticism with the devastating force of a knee in the groin! - many female Instructors disagree with Wrassebender's view, tending to place discrimination above sexual extortion as being the biggest hurdle that women in diving still face.

In any event it's apparent that if diving is to live up to the claim that it's an activity that can be enjoyed by everyone, regardless of gender, then some drastic action is required.

Leaving to one side compulsory sensitivity training, in which hairy, belching, beer-bellied females with bad attitudes explain the finer points of instructional etiquette to all would-be dive leaders, there's a more realistic alternative.

Appreciating that the ability to dive is a gift made more precious when we respect the rights and feelings of others let's encourage the 'hands-off' approach to teaching - and put sex back in the kitchen where it belongs!

CHAPTER 4
FEE, PHY, HO, HUM

Making the grade in today's diving world is becoming increasingly more difficult. It's no longer sufficient to rely on that tatty old neoprene wet suit held together by faith and patches, or wistful tales of, *"When I were down an 'undred feet or more ..."* Now, without a distinctive field of interest, divers are doomed to remain on the outer edge of a fragmented activity dominated by technocrats and specialists.

Sadly the joy and thrill of simply being underwater is, for many, no longer an end in itself. Advances in equipment technology have pushed back the boundaries, in the process paving the way for a new breed of divers who regard their particular sphere of interest as being the only legitimate diving activity and who, all too often, disdainfully ignore those among us who fail to share their passion.

Where conversation among divers at social gatherings once focussed on the total diving experience, the pattern has now changed. There's still talk, of course, about diving in general or the relative merits of particular destinations, but all of that has become little more than an appetiser for the sublime topic of *'Special Interests'*.

Underwater photographers talk about exposure tables, bracketing and the like; marine biologists prattle on about the exciting social life of coral polyps; and 'Technical' Divers, (the amoeba of the diving world) divide into hostile sub-groups broadly categorised by: Cave Divers - an elitist group of equipment "junkies" who, when not wriggling around in small holes, preach the importance of correct gear configuration: Trimix divers - who measure experience by the number of stainless steel 'D'-rings on their BCD's and who, after several beers, will explain to you the most appropriate method of off-gassing any tissue in the body; and Rebreather divers - who sit out on diving's leading edge arguing the toss about the size of their breathing bags. Even Deep Air Divers gather into defensive groups and manage the occasional mumble or glassy-eyed twitch.

The remainder, those of us without a "speciality", become bewildered, stutter a lot, and wonder whether we could ever have really enjoyed our diving without the benefit of such esoteric interests or knowledge.

The major problem, however, in acquiring a special interest is that of cost. It can be expensive and time consuming. And if, like me, you have no real desire to go frolicking around in underwater caves or spending hours at a time on a decompression bar but just want to enjoy diving for its own sake, then it may seem to be a pointless exercise.

It's not! Now that the inmates have taken over the asylum it's imperative that all we 'normal' divers become experts in obscure, ocean related topics. I, for example, aware of my own inadequacies and with a strong desire to be, (providing it costs me nothing) a meaningful contributor to all future conversations with divers, recently decided to become a phycologist! (It surprised me to learn just how many of my former friends – misinterpreting my pronunciation - believed that I already was one!)

A 'phycologist' is, of course, an expert on sea-weeds. A quick glance through Dr Hermione Catfolly's classic work, *'A Lay-Person's Guide To Phycology'* and I'd mastered sufficient terminology to get me past the, *"And what's your particular diving interest?"* stage of any conversation.

I now know that sea-weeds are algae, structurally simple plants that fall into three groups most easily determined by their colour; red [Rhodophyta], brown [Phaeophyta], or green [Chlorophyta], with a less important fourth group consisting of blue-green algae [Cyanophyta]. Providing food and shelter for vertebrates and invertebrates alike, seaweeds are an integral part of the food chain and, being chemically rich, have been harvested by man for centuries, for use as fertiliser, medicine and food.

As a speciality, 'phycology' may not rank as one of the all time diving greats, but as a guaranteed gob-stopper for future non-meaningful chatter with a hearing impaired mixed-gas guru it'll do just fine. Providing there isn't a real Fu ... Fu ... Phycologist around!

CHAPTER 5
A PICTURE'S WORTH A THOUSAND NERDS

Glossy travel brochures never prepare a person for the downside of a diving holiday. One week you're a free spirit, the tang of salt wafting in your nostrils as you roam the oceans of the world; the next you're doing battle with traffic jams and the need to hold hearth and home together by balancing budgets; a sudden shift in focus that takes the lustre out of everyday living.

With no adequate preparation to help overcome the intense pleasure and excitement associated with a diving holiday, the return home can be a stressful experience. For some people it may take months to recover their equilibrium and get their lives back on track.

My friend Krabbmann is a perfect example of this disorder. Every year he takes a two week diving holiday; and every year, upon his return, his work and personal relationships suffer while he puts his life under the microscope. Slowly, as the diving inspired images fade from his mind, he claws his way back to reality only to discover that, exhausted by melancholy, he's in need of another holiday!

The truth is that holidays (and diving holidays in particular) have, for people like Krabbmann, become a vicious cycle from which there is no let up or escape, one that, rather than enriching their daily lives is making it far less tolerable.

Coping with the post-holiday 'blues' isn't easy, despite the advice dished out by well intentioned travel writers who have no idea of the joy or discipline imposed when living out of a damp dive-bag.

They'll tell you to gradually come down to earth from your holiday high by: Deferring the unpacking for a day or so - Not a good idea! The pong from damp dive booties left to ferment for even a short while defies the imagination!; by eating out at restaurants for the first few nights following your return - It's surprising how few restaurants have dress codes that tolerate diners wearing swimming costumes and 'T'-shirts!; how you shouldn't alienate your workmates by bragging about your holiday experiences - Hah! As though any of them have ever hung on the edge of a deep wall while schooling hammerhead sharks circled above their head!; or - and possibly the worst piece of advice - how you should pick up a brochure from the travel agent and begin planning the next holiday; a handy hint that's guaranteed to slow down the recovery process. Not yet properly assimilated back into society and the post holiday syndrome patient is already being urged to plan an escape from it.

Offering, at best, temporary relief and doing nothing to assist rehabilitation back into the work force, advice such as this fails to address the real needs of diving holidaymakers hooked on excitement, adventure and the thrill of discovery.

These folk need to feel warm and fuzzy at the prospect of returning home. Something they're not going to feel like doing after a week or more spent diving magnificent, out-of-the-way, pinnacles and atolls from the comfort of a live-aboard dive vessel, or while exploring the reefs and wrecks of isolated lagoons surrounding remote tropical island resorts.

Short of spending each holiday at a diving destination noted for its inhospitable weather; cold, rough seas filled with highly venomous marine life, and where the operators are brutish morons whose diving equipment is bound together with masking tape, (places that make home, however squalid and humble, seem attractive!), there are, regrettably, few pieces of worthwhile advice to help smooth the transition between play and work.

There is, however, one tactic that's guaranteed to make you appreciate the benefits of home. Known in dive tourism circles as, *'The Wizard of Oz Gambit'*, (or WOG, for short) the remedy is simple. Whenever you go on holiday take with you lots of photographs of your house, spouse/lover, favourite armchair, car, pet goldfish, your office desk, fellow employees, preferred restaurants and even pictures of the quarry where you dive each Sunday.

Take every opportunity to show fellow divers your photographs and bore them incessantly with accompanying background stories to each picture. After a day or so they will have you convinced that, "There's no place like home, Toto! There's no place like home!"

CHAPTER 6
PARDON ME, MYTH, MY NARCOSIS IS SHOWING

Encompassing disciplines like physics, physiology and marine biology, it's little wonder that diving has become fallow ground for the wealth of fables that surface around it.

On a par with urban legends, (like the alligators supposedly dwelling in the sewers of New York city that occasionally clamber up through the plumbing to feed on family pets – or bite the unwary on the bum!), diving myths rely on the same mix of ingredients for their success; a little fact to seal over the cracks and a generous dollop of credible fiction to make the stories worth repeating and to leave the listener wondering if - just maybe - they're true?

One of the better known tales that regularly makes the rounds is that of the diver and the bushfire that goes something like: "Officials searching the area after a huge forest fire ravaged several thousand hectares of countryside surrounding (insert city or town of choice), were shocked to discover the badly burned body of a man wearing a mask, wet-suit, oxygen cylinder (sic) and fins. It is believed that the body was that of a diver who, while enjoying a dive with friends at nearby (insert name of nearest body of water), was inadvertently scooped up into the holding tanks of a fire-fighting aircraft that subsequently dropped its water cargo - including the unwilling passenger - directly into the path of the blaze. "

A more bizarre but equally plausible story concerns spontaneous combustion, a phenomenon in which victims are suddenly reduced to a pile of ashes by an intense heat source that leaves nearby objects and witnesses unharmed. (I know it sounds like 'X-Files' stuff. But I'm serious!). In this particular tale a technical diver who had just completed a deep, mixed gas dive at (insert ocean of choice) was breathing pure oxygen to hasten the decompression process at his final 3-metre stop. Clipped, like his three companions, onto the deco bar for comfort during the lengthy decompression schedule, the diver showed himself to be well and at ease. A second later he was enveloped in a blinding white flash of light. All that remained of the diver was his equipment and empty but intact dry suit that, on internal examination back on the boat, revealed nothing other than a residue of grey, powdery ash.

'Monsters of the Deep' stories occupy a sub-section all to themselves in the litany of diving fables. Given greater credibility by being prefaced with the phrase, "If I hadn't seen it with my own eyes, I'd never have believed it!" these yarns usually revolve around a personal encounter with a giant squid, octopus or shark that's ten times bigger than the norm. "The ancient freighter lay at a depth of 38-metres with a gaping hole on the port side. Determined to explore the ship's interior I approached the hole just as a large grouper prepared to enter. Shining the light from my torch ahead of me, I managed to stop just as the jaws of a huge shark clamped around the unfortunate grouper. The shark must have entered the wreck as a juvenile and spent it's life feeding

- and growing - on the abundant fish life attracted to the stricken vessel. Now, too big to exit through the opening, it waited for prey to swim into its cavernous mouth!"

Good for aprés-dive conversation fillers, most anecdotes of this type are improbable and harmless pieces of fun told at the expense of a gullible listener.

Harder to swallow are the myths being perpetuated by a handful of prominent divers to the effect that all that's needed to overcome the Laws of Physics is 'proper' training. Promoting deep, deep *air* diving way beyond the accepted recreational limits, these folk will have you believe that they are immune to the effects of nitrogen narcosis and oxygen toxicity. Rejecting the rigid principles of science, they ask only that would be students open their minds - and pockets! - to their teachings.

Although more deadly in the consequences these people display the same irrational thought processes as the boat skipper who followed a pair of drift divers across the international dateline. When the divers surfaced the skipper insisted that the pair had exceeded their 40-minutes bottom time by 24-hours and immediately put them in the deck decompression chamber for extended treatment.

"If I hadn't seen it with my own eyes, I'd never have believed it!"

CHAPTER 7
HERE THERE BE MONSTERS - AND BUGS

The makers of ancient navigational charts had it easy! Whenever they ran out of information on the boundaries of the known world they just scrawled quick and convenient warnings like, "Here there be Monsters", around the edges of their maps before poddling off to the local Cartographers Club for a beer with their mates.

With few entrepreneurs prepared to underwrite the costly risk of exploration beyond the known limits there were no requirements to write more detailed explanations like, "I'm sorry but I don't really know if there's anything worth visiting beyond this point but I don't think that there is so you're really better off not bothering to find out but if you insist on doing so then it's your problem not mine."

Diving into the internet is similar to putting to sea with one of those early charts. You never know what you may discover, or whether you'll return unscathed! (Even the "Monsters" have only undergone a minor upgrade to "Virus" status.)

Now just a mouse-click away from the computer screen,

information on every aspect of diving is closer and, for many internet users, more convenient than a visit to the local dive shop.

Usually accompanied by stunning graphics and a wealth of mind-boggling material, some sites are as huge and varied as big city department stores - and equally well stocked with goodies that you didn't realise a need for until you accidentally stumbled across them.

Others - particularly the thousands of home pages maintained by individual divers - are like market stalls where, if you devote sufficient time and patience to rummaging through the bric-a-brac, you're bound to find something of value. Rarely repaying the time and effort spent in searching for them, however, many of these treasures only come to light after wading through pages of gibberish and dank tales littered with phrases like, "We sank down through the azure blue, our bubbles drifting above us like a silver screen as we descended onto the pristine reef below." (No one, it seems, ever enjoys diving on reefs that are less than 'pristine'!)

The problem is that with hundreds of thousands of sites devoted to scuba diving alone, a journey through cyber space can be as unpredictable as diving in the middle of a shark-run with a dead mackerel strapped to each fin - or a midnight stroll through a bad part of town while clutching a wad of fifty-dollar bills! Take the wrong path while looking for information on wet-suits and you may wind up in out-of-the-way places with names like, "Naughty Nina's Rubber Dungeon"! Obscure locations filled with the ever present risk of contracting bugs and viruses that you won't find mentioned in any diving manual!

Even restricting your internet activities to talking about diving is fraught with risk. Pick a diving related topic - from underwater photography through to hyperbaric medicine or rebreather technology - and the chances are that there's a specialised e-mail newsgroup providing opportunities for people in countries as far apart as Finland and Patagonia to air their views, opinions and prejudices.

Not recommended for the sensitive or faint of heart some forums, particularly those dealing with the more esoteric aspects of technical diving, are notorious for the ferocity of their debates and the savage, often uncomfortable and physically impossible responses that follow questions like, "Where should I stick my snorkel when cave diving?"

Reduced to words on a computer screen - and with none of the inhibitions imposed when physically confronting a 250-pound giant who adds emphasis to each dogmatic opinion by smacking one clenched fist into the palm of the other while looking you straight in the eye - there's a low signal-to-noise ratio; a lot of talk with very little substance and all of it passing around the world in just seconds. And anyone can play! "Hey! I'm a Doctor and my research shows that the absorption of nitrogen into the tissues of the body is slowed dramatically after ingesting a handful of roast coffee beans followed by 10-minutes immersion in a bath of gin." Great news if you happen to have shares in a distillery but otherwise of doubtful value.

The sad fact is that the internet is strong on information and light on wisdom, whereas a trip to the local dive shop usually reveals the opposite: A limited choice of regulators (all of which are probably made by the same OEM!) but with a wealth of acquired diving knowledge, a place where any bugs that you might catch can usually be cured with an aspirin!

CHAPTER 8
JUST WHEN YOU THOUGHT IT WAS SAFE

Mike Nelson would have scoffed at dive industry statistics suggesting that diving is safer than netball, bee keeping or bowling! In his day diving was dangerous!

During more than 150 episodes of the weekly television series, "Sea Hunt", he battled the bends and embolisms; decimated the world's shark population; pillaged sunken wrecks; plunged to hitherto unheard of depths trialing new diving equipment; and kept the oceans of the 'free' world safe from underwater saboteurs and spies - usually by slicing through their air hoses with a knife during the rough and tumble of hand-to-hand underwater combat!

As the star of the pioneering series, (in which he played the role of 'Mike Nelson', former navy diver turned underwater explorer), veteran actor, Lloyd Bridges - who died early in 1998 - became an instrumental figure in popularising scuba diving during the late 'fifties and early 'sixties.

He achieved this not by suggesting that Scuba diving is, 'Fun', 'Enjoyable' or 'Safe', (terms that have come into common useage in an attempt to broaden recreational diving's appeal) nor by highlighting the natural wonders of the undersea world. For Mike Nelson, each dive was a high-risk challenge fraught with danger.

Inspired by his small screen adventures, tens of thousands of people from around the world came to regard scuba diving as the ultimate adrenalin activity.

Following the rush to learn the basic principles of diving, either through clubs, or by reading one of the 'teach-yourself' text books then available, many of those people went on to become influential figures in the way that diving is now marketed; forgetting, with the passage of time, what it was that had first attracted them to diving; a sea-change in attitude that's hastened the spread of car bumper stickers with messages like, "I remember when sex was safe and diving was dangerous!"

A quarter of a century after Lloyd Bridges hung up his twin-hose regulator, television producers decided that it was time to capitalise on the success of the original "Sea Hunt" series. Casting a former television, 'Tarzan' in the starring role they ignored the winning formula of the earlier show.

Instead of the vinegary, Lloyd Bridges' character, ("You only know you're alive when your air supply gives out!"), the 'new', Mike Nelson was a sensitive person who laboured the importance of proper training, pre-dive safety drills, the buddy system and the need for environmental conservation. He probably never peed in his wet-suit and the only time he ever drew his knife was to free an enmeshed dolphin or to remove coral fragments from the flipper of a lame turtle!

It was such a sanitised interpretation of the original series that the programme quickly disappeared, with scarcely a ripple to mark its passing!

In private, a number of Training Organisations admit that in selling diving as a 'safe' activity that can be quickly learned by almost everybody, they have trivialised the potential risks and overlooked the importance of 'excitement' as a marketing tool.

Sitting at home on a couch watching television is 'safe', (unless you happen to switch channels while your partner's watching a football game with the scores drawn and only two minutes to go to the final whistle. Then it becomes 'thrilling'!) whereas drift-diving along a sheer wall in the middle of a shark run or penetrating a previously unexplored wreck is 'exhilarating'.

Glossing over the inherent danger in diving doesn't make it any more appealing, nor is it in the best interests of those people who - having completed an entry level course and clutching a certification card that never expires - feel that they have no need for advanced or continuous diving training. *("I've done that! Now I'm going to add some real fizz to my life and take up lawn bowls.")*

Diving doesn't have to deny its excellent record for safety in order to sell itself as an adrenalin-activity second to none. Neither does it need to revert back to the dark old days when Instructors would tell students, *"Pay attention to what I say or you will die, horribly and painfully!"* to add spice to its image.

It does, however, need to rid itself of the embarrassing notion that it's safer than netball! Mike Nelson would have lent his full support to a campaign of that sort.

CHAPTER 9
ALL A-BORED

It begins the moment that some people step across the gangway of a live-aboard dive vessel; a character make-over that turns them from previously considerate and well-mannered divers into salty sea-dogs who - often without realising it - manage to bore the booties off of passengers and crew alike.

Ranging from the mildly insensitive to the gratingly obnoxious, 'Liveaboard Bores' are the dark side of what should be one of diving's most sublime and enjoyable experiences. While some (like me) remain blissfully unaware of their own character defects, others take advantage of the fact that, in the confines of a small vessel, they have a captive audience.

The types vary. There are those who immediately commandeer the best cabin or bunk while you're busy ingratiating yourself with the most important person aboard - the cook.

Others suffer a sea-change in terms of their language. Suddenly acquiring an accent like Long John Silver's - and while the boat's still firmly moored to the jetty - they'll say things like, "Ah! It's good to feel a heaving deck beneath one's feet again."

These are the same people who insist on referring to the pointed end of the boat as the 'bow' and lace every conversation with plenty of, 'larboards', 'starboards' and other sailor-talk. Ask one of them for directions to the bathroom and you're likely to be told, "Harrr! Harrr! Me Hearty! The Heads be abaft the galley flat, just below the poop-deck." (a piece of advice that has been known to cause acute embarrassment to those unfamiliar with nautical terminology.)

Then there are those who - when the seas are a little choppy and you're still waiting for your stomach to return to its proper position and acquire sea-legs of its own - will insist on giving you a blow-by-blow account of every live-aboard dive boat that they've been on while chomping into a greasy snack.

"I remember a time, (it was out in the South China Sea during a typhoon), when the skipper - at my suggestion - lashed all of the women passengers to the mast! With the main engines broken down and heavy beam seas threatening to capsize the vessel, I saved the day by rigging a sea-anchor out of one of my smelly old socks stuffed full of butter from the galley."

Turning bright green around the gills in the face of an impending vomit attack is no deterrent either. *"Then there was the time that my buddies and I chartered an old pilchard boat to dive some deep wrecks. It was great! Everybody but me got bent. And the food was superb; raw onions, tinned herrings in tomato sauce and suet and treacle pudding. Oh! My! You're really not feeling at all well, are you? Personally, I've never suffered from sea-sickness."*

But it's on the diving deck that the worst category of, 'Live-aboard Bores' really make their on-board presence felt. Easily recognised in their more extreme form by their faded, *"I Dived The Titanic"* T-shirts, these folk are driven by a need to prove their diving superiority.

Before the dive they'll happily embarrass you by loudly explaining why it is that every piece of diving equipment that you own is obsolete, badly configured and incapable of sustaining intelligent life.

After the dive they'll point up the flaws in your finning technique, scoff at your poor air consumption, your conservative attitude to depth and time and then tell you that they've dived deeper and for longer in weather so foul that even whales wouldn't put to sea.

It's towards the end of the trip that they usually say something like:

"You wimps don't know what you're doing. Join me on your next vacation and I'll show you some "real" diving."

Faced with this proposal, Krabbmann has the perfect answer, *"Maybe!"* he responds, " *But don't forget the first rule of diving."*

"What's that?" They invariably ask.

"Don't hold your breath!" is his response.

Fortunately bores of this calibre are a rarity. But should you find yourself kitting up next to one, take the initiative and crush several garlic oil capsules into their wet suit booties at the end of the diving day.

As you prepare for the next dive, loudly screech:

"Phew! Hasn't anybody ever told you the value of personal hygiene

and the importance of caring for your equipment? Speak to me later and I'll give you some tips."

Chances are, they'll avoid you for the rest of the trip.

CHAPTER 10
MINDING YOUR P'S IN Q'S

None of the Training Agencies seem to deal effectively with the peculiarities of diving etiquette or how to handle socially awkward moments. As far as they're concerned they've done their duty in teaching the social niceties by tagging entry-level courses with vague statements like, "Remember to respect the rights of others!" before casting newly certified divers adrift to fend for themselves.

Bearing in mind that, "Good Manners are the glue that binds the fabric of society together." - a useful phrase to remember when somebody is openly critical of your decision to wear a snorkel! – it is important to recognise that conventional etiquette does nothing to prepare a person for what, in diving, passes as 'civilised' behaviour.

What you wear, for instance, is less important than *how* it's worn. Take facemasks: Wearing a mask up on your forehead while on the surface is considered bad form. (Unless you happen to be a Deep Air diver, in which case the mask may be worn back to front with the mask strap - because of the cranial slope - passing low across the forehead no higher than one inch above the single joined eyebrow.)

Similarly, *What* you do is less important than *how* you do it! For those people who still prefer to de-fog their mask with saliva rather than using one of the commercial preparations, the correct method is to turn your back on bystanders and, with the action coming from the mouth alone, gently spit directly onto the mask lens with a noise no louder than a soft, "Phwittt!". (A spitting action drawn from the back of the throat or from deep down in the toes and culminating in an explosive, "AAHHRRRRGPHWEWPH!" is considered unnecessary and nothing more than an ostentatious attempt to impress others with your prowess.)

Neither is it always appropriate to offer assistance to those divers less gifted than one's self. Remember - an offer to spit into somebody else's facemask will often create a dilemma for the owner.

An uncouth diver may be tempted to respond to such an offer by saying something like,

"What? You're joking, aren't you? You've still got bits of spinach from dinner stuck between your teeth!"

But, the well mannered diver understands that a soft rejection is less likely to cause offence. Their answer would probably follow the lines of:

"That's terribly kind of you, but I actually plan to work on my mask clearing technique by allowing it to fog and periodically letting in water to cleanse it. Perhaps another time?"

With few direct parallels to draw on, novice divers are usually ill-prepared to handle the devastating effects of cold water and pressure.

Helping a person to maintain their dignity when - on surfacing - you notice that a minor sinus problem has transferred itself to their face requires finesse. As does explaining to them that it's not always necessary to cut short a dive because they get caught short.

It's highly unlikely that anyone standing in a bus queue on a cold day would think to themselves, *"Ah. I'll just warm myself up a bit by having a pee in my trousers."* but many divers see nothing untoward or shameful in having a whiz in their wet-suit.

Although this is not something that is actively encouraged, there are, nevertheless, established protocols in place regarding the practice. It should, for example, never be attempted unless already in the water. And it is considered bad manners to pee in any suit other than your own. A constraint often ignored by the socially inept. (Yet another convincing reason to rush out and buy a suit of your own). And if you really value the goodwill of your fellow divers, remember to wash it immediately after the dive - preferably with a deodorising anti-bacterial wash. Simply leaving your suit to dry in the sun will not only tarnish your image, but that of anything else with which it comes into contact.

Although the idea would probably be pooh-pooh'd by the Training Agencies, there's a lot to be said for making a course in Diving Etiquette a pre-requisite for all Instructor candidates. After all, who wants to be taught the art of undressing or how to spit by somebody who drinks beer, belches and scratches a lot and tries to command respect by mumbling things like, *"Trust me Monica. I'm a diving Instructor!"*

CHAPTER 11
TANKS FOR THE MEMORIES

Never believe folks who tell you that nostalgia doesn't have a future: There's a lot to be learned from the past. Particularly with regard to diving and the common misconception that 'experience' is a measure of how long a person's been doing something rather than a gauge of any knowledge gained.

Based on the fact that there are, today, almost as many active divers in their forties, fifties and sixties as there are in the younger age groups, the local dive store recently initiated a scheme intended to get older divers back into the water and bridge the generation gap.

The idea - to show that physical age is no barrier to a person's enjoyment of diving - had its genesis in the front bar of, "The Sozzled Cod", a notorious hang-out for a group of chronological misfits who, for the price of a glass of warm milk, will tell anybody who cares to listen about their early diving exploits.

Unlike most of their peers in diving who have willingly embraced diving's new technology and gracefully surrendered to the passing years by adopting a more conservative attitude to time and depth, this particular group remained unaware of the meaningful developments in diving since they first took up the activity back in the late 'fifties or early 'sixties.

Equipment proved the first sticking point in the plan.

"You paid how much for your gear? Why, when I were a young 'un, you could outfit yourself with top of the range gear for less than three hundred dollars - and still have money left over to buy replacement ping-pong balls for your snorkel.

"My Aqua-lung - a 70 cu. ft. tank with harness, twin-hose regulator and a reserve valve - cost me just $160.00, and it's still working. Of course, divers were tougher and fitter in those days, so we never had to worry about dive tables or decompression sickness. It was impossible to get bent doing a single dive!

"Mind you. I always kept track of depth with my wrist depth gauge that read to 220 feet. That set me back $2.45, but it was worth it for the peace of mind. Waste of time having other gauges. In any case you always knew when it was time to come up because breathing became difficult. Tell you what: Why don't you borrow my gear for tomorrow's dive?"

Showing signs of already crumbling around the edges, the scheme was finally scrapped on the following day when the divers detailed to buddy with the three old 'crustaceans' refused to get in the water with them.

"I didn't object to the equipment that they planned to use - mostly heavy-duty black rubber." Said Lisa, one of the volunteer divemasters. *"Nor the fact that it took them twice as long as everybody else to gear up while they struggled into home-made wet-suits*

constructed of unlined neoprene held together with glue, tape and faith.

"And as for all the talcum powder that they smothered themselves and everything else in the immediate vicinity with", she continued, "well ... at least it made them smell better even if it did cake itself over everybody else's gear.

"I didn't even object to the fact that all three of them refused to wear a BCD; that one of them wanted to carry a speargun with powerhead, "in case we met a shark"; that they didn't have a single contents gauge between them; nor that their dive plan was to go in and dive deep until it was time to tug the reserve lever on their old 'J' valves and ascend.

"No! The thing that really got to me was their insistence on showing everybody the kinks in their hoses and the wrinkles in their fabric - proof, they claimed, of plenty of 'hands-on' experience. Now that was disgusting!"

Back at their normal place in the bar, the three showed themselves to be unrepentant.

"These youngsters don't know anything, do they? And what's really sad about today is that one of them threw my flippers over the side of the boat."

"Not your 'Frankie Golden Flippers'?"

"Yep! Set me back $2.95, when I bought them in 1955. Don't know where I'll lay my hands on another pair like those."

It's true what they say, isn't it? 'Fins – and fings - ain't what they used to be!

CHAPTER 12
AN IMAGE WORTH FRAMING

When asked what underwater activity they would most like to learn many divers nominate underwater photography. It's easy to understand why.

An intense experience filled with colour, light and movement, diving is an adventure that's best captured by images rather than words. Sadly - for those unable to invest the time and money in acquiring the expertise - the most exciting and memorable moments remain nothing more than memories that dull with passing time.

Achieving success in underwater photography isn't easy. Quite apart from the need to master essential technical skills, amphibious photographers have to contend with malicious claims by detractors that they:

- Are conceited and insensitive.
- Have an inflated opinion of their diving abilities.

- Have no understanding of teamwork, the buddy system or its purpose.
- Resent the underwater presence of other divers.
- Think nothing of crawling across fragile coral architecture in an attempt to capture on film a rare creature that's in danger of extinction because of environmental damage to its habitat.
- Remove creatures from their natural haunts in order to photograph them in more attractive surroundings.
- And that they are only motivated by the desire for reward and recognition!

With allegations like these constantly being levelled against them, underwater photographers have become their own worst enemies. Focussed only on what appears in the viewfinder of a camera - a preoccupation that is sometimes mistaken for rudeness - they often neglect the social niceties and fail to make the general diving public aware of the personal cost of being bitten by the shutter-bug, or what it entails.

It's a reputation that is ill deserved - almost all the underwater photographers of my acquaintance are modest, friendly and fun to dive with. The sort of people, in fact, who usually remember to say, "Thank you!" when a fellow live-aboard passenger is obliged to give up their bunk and sleep on the deck in order to make room for the photographer's excess camera equipment, and who never hesitate to give freely of their knowledge and time in helping less gifted novices get a foothold on the ladder to diving fame and fortune.

. . .

An example of this benevolence is the advice that I received from the local Underwater Photographic Society when I applied for membership.

Although my application was rejected, (probably because I answered the question, "Why do you wish to join?" with, "To get my snout into the prize trough!", rather than the more appropriate, "To advance my knowledge and understanding of underwater photography!"), they did offer some useful tips on getting started.

The first requirement is, of course, a camera. It apparently doesn't matter what brand of camera that you buy providing that it costs lots of money and comes with a full range of matching accessories. Apart from the fact that a really, really expensive underwater camera marks you as a professional, the amount of money outlaid is proportional to the perception that others have of your creative ability. After all, why would anyone spend so much on costly equipment unless they had the artistic talent to use it all properly?

Once you've become familiar with the knobs and buttons, mastered the art of removing the lens cover and taken several thousand images, it's time to give thought to a portfolio.

It sounds easy enough to put together a selection of your best work when you have several thousand images to choose from, but if you want to stay in the race for a competition prize or Award then the portfolio *must* include pictures of:

. . .

1) A young and attractive female model – with heavy eye make-up – peering through a single-lens face-mask at a small and inoffensive marine animal. (Do not include pictures of ageing, ugly, or overweight divers; people with old or uncoordinated diving equipment; or divers who are not smiling.)

2) A shark, with jaws wide open, swimming straight towards the camera. (Wherever possible the photographer should try and convey the impression that each image entails extreme personal risk!)

3) A clown fish emerging from the tentacles of a sea-anemone. (This shot demonstrates a preparedness to spend weeks at a time – the generosity of liveaboard operators permitting! – diving the world's hot spots in search of this rare creature!)

Although they made no mention of creative technique, the Society's Membership Committee were adamant that by following their advice even a novice, such as myself, would soon be able to offer their members some stiff competition.

Even the required financial outlay was, they said, no obstacle. Yesterday they offered me paid work modelling diving equipment for one of their members. It's apparently to photograph the prototype of a new all-lead diving suit intended for use by divers working in nuclear power plants!

CHAPTER 13
THE LITTLE SHOP OF HORRORS

Going diving is heaps more fun than monitoring the marketing pages of the business press, but if some diving operators hope to keep their heads above water then they may need to catch up on their reading.

Obsessed with teaching diving - probably because it's the only aspect of the diving business that they actually understand - a few instructors and dive store owners continue to regard the certification process as an end in itself rather than the first step in building long term customer relationships.

Pitching diving against the instant gratification culture of fast foods and bungy jumping, they make no attempt to *sell* and *promote* it as a unique, equipment intensive, adventure activity with rewards that more than repay the time spent in learning.

Opting instead for the line of least resistance they heavily discount the price of courses and place a continuing reliance on slogans like, "Learning to dive has never been easier!" (A strange claim when we all know that it takes at least four days just to master the underwater hand signals for saying, *"I'm cold! I have serious doubts about the quality of your rental equipment and this is the sixth time we have swum past this abandoned supermarket trolley! When will I be exposed to the fun, the excitement and the exotic marine life as promised in the glossy promotional brochure that you handed to me when I first enquired about diving?")*

There are lots of reasons for this attitude. But the most common is that a handful of instructors and dive shop owners still regard diving as an alternative lifestyle rather than a business.

Oblivious to the need for profit and customer service, their shop premises usually reflect a poverty of thought and pocket that keeps the business constantly teetering on the brink of financial ruin.

Not that their stores are ever empty. Like *'R Gang's Klubhouse'*, there's usually at least half-a-dozen 'dive-shop groupies' with names like "Buggalugs" and "Zombie", always hanging around drinking coffee, telling implausible tales about near-death underwater experiences and loudly advising would-be customers that the regulator they were thinking of buying is $17.56 cents cheaper at a shop on the other side of town.

With insufficient turnover to afford professional, service-oriented staff - and a need to maintain cash-flow by teaching courses - some dive operators tolerate the presence of folk like these because of their willingness to, "mind the store for a few days", without pay. An act of folly that helps prove that although learning to dive might be easy, actually going diving once you're certified is an altogether different kettle of kippers!

I stumbled across this practice recently when, following the advice given to divers of always seeking an orientation to new diving areas, I telephoned a local dive store:

"Hello! I'm planning a week-end dive trip for a large group and I'd like some preliminary information on your area"

"You've come to the right place. We've got some of the best diving in the world! You must have heard of Apocalypse Reef. It's where the offshore sewage outlet empties. Even on a bad day, you can find things floating around out there that you'll never see anywhere else!"

"What about boat dives?"

"Every day regardless of the sea conditions. Except at the moment. Last week one of our divers fired his spear-gun through the RIB's inflation tube and the owner, Jack, hasn't got around to patching it yet - but usually every day!"

"What about hire equipment?"

"Right at the moment, Jack's using both sets on a course that he's teaching. But we've got a few bits and pieces of second-hand gear for sale."

"And what's the best time of the year to dive in your area?"

"Ah! Now that's a good question, isn't it? Jack's the best person to answer that and he's out diving at the moment. Why don't you call him back sometime next week. Make it in the morning, though. He's not usually sober after lunch!"

It's almost as if some dive operators are genuinely concerned by the thought that if every certified diver in the world elected to go diving on the same day and at the same time, then the global rise in sea levels might cause devastating coastal flooding. And that, of course, would put them out of business!

CHAPTER 14
I DID IT MY WEIGH

Few of us pay as much attention to our diving health and fitness as we should. I made this discovery while looking into a dive shop window recently.

With my nose pressed to the glass - and oblivious to everything other than the exciting new gizmos and gadgets on display - I suddenly became aware that the owner was staring back at me and making shooing signs with his hands. (Apparently I was smudging his windowpane and frightening away the customers.)

Stepping back from the window, I noticed that the same store owner, (a person whom I'd always considered to be, *'well padded'*), was standing framed entirely within the outline of my own reflection - with plenty of room to spare.

It came as a rude shock to realise that the discomfort I've been experiencing squeezing into my wetsuit had more to do with my 'few' extra pounds in weight gain rather than because - as I'd been claiming - the neoprene was shrinking!

"Not that there's anything wrong with having a few additional layers of thermal insulation." I told people. (In a vain attempt to justify a physique that had become increasingly in need of a good makeover.) "Take whales, for example. Their land-based ancestors were probably scrawny critters with a liking for fish who managed to evolve into creatures perfectly adapted to staying warm in the cold aquatic environment. And look at the trade-off for carting around a ton or two of surplus blubber: The ability to dive to incredible depths for extended periods of time; an underwater speed and grace that belies their bulk; and enormously popular with underwater photographers."

(For those folk who appreciate the difference in physiology between homo sapiens and whales, the flaws in this comparison are obvious. To the best of my knowledge there has never been one recorded instance of a fat whale contracting decompression illness - and overweight divers *never* feature in underwater photographs!)

It's something of a paradox that despite our better understanding of underwater physics and physiology since diving pioneers like Gilpatric, Cousteau, Hass and Tailliez, first wrote about their exploits, the general attitude towards diving health and fitness is one of apathy.

Without exception all of the photographs from those early books showed divers who looked, by today's standards, almost painfully thin and undernourished. And while being overweight is only one aspect of whether or not we're as fit for diving as we should be, it's certainly one of the most obvious.

Quite apart from the additional strain on the heart and lungs imposed by all that excess weight, there's a greater susceptibility to decompression sickness and a real need to dramatically reduce bottom times in line with the degree of obesity.

(Not a good thing if you want to keep your diving buddies happy.)

In fact it's suggested that for recreational diving purposes a person should be no greater than 20% above the average ideal weight when taking into consideration age, height and build. Generally speaking this is something that's within our power to remedy through appropriate exercise and proper diet - but preferably accomplished in consultation with a diving physician.

Don't do as I did and rely on advice from a friend. Knowing that I wanted to achieve my physical peak, Krabbmann suggested that I might like to adopt the same training regimen and balanced diet programme as followed by the U.S. Navy SEALS!

I wasn't aware that the U.S. Navy actually had anything to do with training pinnipeds, but as the nearest ones that I knew of were at the local zoo, I went there to watch and take notes.

As far as I could make out the seal training seemed to consist of nothing more than remaining poised on one flipper while balancing a ball on the end of the nose. Although that, in itself, was difficult enough to master, it was the rigid diet that almost caused me to give up on the idea: Just one plastic bucketful of dead pilchards a day!

However, after only three weeks, I'm now able to fit comfortably back into my wetsuit. Not only that, but my hair has become all glossy and shiny and I'm a hit with photographers who keep asking me to pose with a ball on the end of my nose.

It would seem that those Navy SEALS really do know a thing or two!

CHAPTER 15
WRITING A WRONG

Bending the truth a little is an important part of diving culture. As far as I can see there's very little point in doing a dive if, at the end of it, the only entry that you can make in your logbook is, "Got in! Got wet! Got out!"; or – after the umpteenth dive at the same well visited site - "More of the same!"

Even the most mundane dive is a unique adventure that, with just a little embellishment, can achieve the proportions of a science-fiction epic. It's certainly got all of the right ingredients: Travel; technology; hostile environments; alien life-forms; exciting discoveries from ancient civilizations; the constant element of risk - not to mention sex and human interest.

In many log-books these broad headings are translated into something like: "We travelled to the dive site aboard the worthy vessel, the 'Yuppy Guppy'; put on our gear and back-flipped over the side into the water. (That's 'travel', 'technology' and 'hostile environments', attended to). We saw a fish, (alien life-form?), living in an empty beer-bottle, (exciting discoveries from ancient civilizations?). As we were getting low on air, (constant element of risk?), we ascended to our safety stop before climbing back on board the boat. I helped my buddy to undress." (Definitely, 'human interest'!)

It may be a factual account of what happened, but what this record lacks is any riveting detail that, re-reading it in future years, conveys any of the thrill and excitement of that particular day's dive – or the heroic role of the chronicler; (An important aspect of any personal narrative.)

Oftentimes just travelling to a dive site provides sufficient material to spice up any logbook. Take, for example, my recent trip to the island of Cozumel, in Mexico, with an international group of diving adventurers and bon vivants.

Chartering three six-pack dive vessels, each with a crew of three, we set out to dive Maracaibo Reef, a seldom visited dive site to the south of the island. Once clear of the lee of the island, the combined forces of a low swell and choppy sea began to take effect. Our boat trailed behind the other two vessels as my fellow passengers and I decided that our stomachs were in different places to our hearts! Eventually – after much begging and pleading – we convinced our reluctant skipper to turn his boat around and find a more sheltered dive site.

"Admit it, Strike." Said 'Reef Fish' – the group's leader – after his dive at the intended site. "Those little swells at the Maracaibo probably got the adrenaline and stomach juices of those on your boat flowing."

It was true. Mine were almost flowing into the bilges! But history – not to mention personal self-esteem – would be better served, I thought, by a more creative account of the day's events:

"In spite of our discomfort, all aboard our vessel were of one mind! 'Push on! Push on!', we cried out to the skipper.

"'But, Senor Loco, eet is madness. The waves will overpower and sink my small craft. I must turn back for all our sakes, lest we become food for the feeshes!'

"'The sea's no place for girly talk like that!' I yelled. 'Follow in the wake of that other boat, or we'll seize command of this vessel and lash you to the mast along with the wimmin folk.'

"Despite the apparent appeal of this idea – and cries from the ladies that they weren't opposed to it either - he still resisted, putting forward one final and telling argument!

" 'But, Senor Plonker. My T-shirt, eet is getting soggy!'

"His wretched plea touched my soul. I relented, 'Oh, very well then. Turn back to calmer waters if you must!'"

I showed this portion of my logged entry to my companions, all of whom agreed that, with the possible exception of who actually said what – and to whom - it bore vague similarities to their own recollection of events.

After such hesitancy, I was a little loath to let them read my description of the dive itself. Thankfully, however, the true facts are all recorded in the pages of my dive log for anyone to see, a permanent and lasting reminder of enjoyable times, good company and memorable dives. Which is, after all – the whole purpose of keeping a logbook. Isn't it?

CHAPTER 16
SUM FIZZY-OLOGY

It's one of the great mysteries of diving: The number of otherwise seemingly intelligent people who think that physics and physiology have no relevance to their own diving practices.

Claiming that they've, "never been good at science or maths", they've developed a self-imposed 'blind-spot' where their own safety and well-being is concerned.

Ignoring everything that they once learned about the effects of pressure on the human body; the importance of being able to calculate depth and time; and all of the contributing factors to Decompression Sickness, they gladly surrender all responsibility to somebody whom they believe to be more experienced than themselves – or to a Dive Computer.

Invite these people to use a set of dive tables and manually calculate their No-Decompression Limits, or their residual nitrogen obligations when planning subsequent dives, and they go all goggle-eyed, splutter and gasp like a stranded fish and tell you how – apart from that one gap in their knowledge – just how good and experienced a diver they are.

On the other hand, ask them to quickly open a bottle of fizzy soft drink that's been left in the heat of the sun for several hours before being violently shaken and they'd laugh in your face and probably say something like, "Huh. You must think I'm stupid. It'll spray all over the place and stain my new white shirt!"

They may not necessarily understand the mechanics of why it happens – but observation and experience has convinced them that there's a strong probability that it will!

These are the same folks who happily entrust their health and safety to the care of a stranger - but not their appearance and pride; and as for any claims about their supposed inability to 'do sums', just watch them when they go into a supermarket to buy their week's groceries. They know to the exact cent how much they should pay, and woe betide any shop assistant who overcharges or short-changes them!

Paradoxically those same people seldom quibble, (or check the dive tables for themselves), when a Dive Master says something like, "This next dive is to 20-metres with a maximum bottom time of 45-minutes." Not that they actually comprehend the advice. Thanks to the widespread use of dive computers there's now a growing dependency on technology.

But instead of treating these instruments as useful tools that require at least a little appreciation and understanding of the causes of decompression sickness, many users regard them as infallible talismans that will protect them from harm: rather like carrying the underwater equivalent of a 'lucky' rabbit's foot!

That was certainly the case with one diver that we spotted

leaning over the side of the vessel, apparently fishing, following the first dive of a recent liveaboard trip.

"Caught anything?" I asked.

"What? Oh ... No - I didn't pay attention to the dive plan and overstayed my bottom time during that first dive. According to the computer, I was supposed to carry out a 2-minute decompression stop. But after all the beer that I drank on-shore last night, I wasn't feeling too good so I surfaced straight away. Now I've got my computer dangling on the end of the line 'decompressing'. I'll leave it there for another 10-minutes just to be on the safe side!"

As though the possible consequences of such frightening ignorance wasn't bad enough, things took a sudden turn for the worse when the thin line snapped.

After cursing and swearing, he calmed down. "Just as well I remembered to pack a spare computer", he said, "otherwise I might have run into difficulties on the next dive."

He might have, too, had he not opened a can of warm beer in front of an amazed Dive Master and been 'grounded' from diving for 24-hours. Now that's something that you *can* depend on!

CHAPTER 17
TRASH OR TREASURE

It might be stamps, stuffed teddy bears, works of art or postcards, but no matter what it is, the chances are that somebody, somewhere has a passion for collecting it.

For some folk it's an appreciation of the perceived beauty or craftsmanship of an item: Others regard their collections as long-term investments that – they hope – will increase in value. Some people restrict themselves to specific categories of 'collectibles', like bank-notes or parking tickets, while others are more broad-ranging in their tastes, collecting anything that serves to remind them of people, places and events that have influenced their lives. For some people collecting becomes an obsession. For others it's a fascinating and usually harmless hobby.

Take a look around at most popular activities and the chances are that they have all developed their own sub-culture involving 'collectibles'. Diving is no exception.

A friend of mine, for example, collects standard diving helmets that he's gathered from around the world. Rescued from use as doorstops, novelty plant-pots or bar lights, he's lovingly restored each of them to working condition and gets as much joy out of actually diving with them as he does from the knowledge that he's helping to preserve a part of diving's history.

Equally driven are those people who scour second-hand bookshops and garage sales for out of print copies of books on diving's early days or back issues of old diving magazines. A practical and inexpensive way of learning more about diving from the trial-and-error mistakes of the past, much of the information that these publications contain still has relevance today.

In some quarters, the certification cards accompanying training programmes are now regarded as collectible items. Based on the assumption that certification cards alone are an indication of diving prowess - and with the sole aim of adding to their collection rather than their knowledge - many people sign up for every specialty diving course on offer: The more esoteric the course, the better.

(Some years ago a popular diving magazine printed an advertisement for an 'Underwater Knife-fighting Course' in the issue coinciding with April Fool's Day. For the obvious reason - as the publisher thought - no contact details were given. The publication was swamped with enquiries from divers wanting to sign up for the course!)

But not everybody collects tangible things! Some divers 'collect' exotic destinations, or live-aboards. In a perpetual quest for that elusive 'best' dive site they travel the world to places that many of us can only dream about, bringing back with them as evidence of their exploits nothing more than a sticker that they slap onto the side of their gear bag to show that they've, "Been there. Dived that!"

(In that regard, I've always favoured 'T'-shirts over stickers as 'collectible' items. Particularly if they're limited in number and carry an exclusive logo with a catchy slogan like the one designed by our friend 'Crusty' for a recent dive trip. Wearing a 'T'-shirt featuring a sombrero-clad, twin-hose breathing, death's head with the motto, *"Cheating Death With Every Breath!"*, gets the one-upmanship message across in a subtle way without the need to alienate people by saying something like, "Nyha, nyanyha, nyanyha! I went diving to Mexico and you didn't!").

Other divers collect wrecks, spending months of research pinpointing the site of a sunken vessel in order to be the first to dive it. Concerned by the fact that once its position is known other less idealistic souls might be tempted into a looting frenzy, many of these wreck hunters take the initiative by arming themselves with a crowbar and removing for safe keeping to their homes things like portholes, binnacles, telegraphs and the ship's bell.

It doesn't matter what it is, if it involves diving then it's almost certain that somebody collects it. Sadly, however, it's not always a harmless pastime. There still exists a small group of divers who insist on bringing back mementos from each of their dives; things like pieces of coral or shells with living creatures still in them.

Ignoring the maxim, "Take only memories. Leave only bubbles.", this miserable collection of trashers truly belong in a museum!

CHAPTER 18
WHAT A GUY

First published in 1934 and widely regarded as the first book to popularise recreational snorkelling and scuba diving, Guy Gilpatric's, "The Compleat Goggler", concludes with, ..."nothing he (man) has ever done has spoiled the bottom of the sea, nor will anything he can ever do leave a lasting trace upon it. ... (But just the same, if I were you, I'd get a pair of goggles and see it while the seeing's good!)"

It was such neat advice that people all around the world rushed out to their tool-shed's and began cobbling together their own snorkelling equipment from whatever materials came to hand. Armed with old aviator goggles lined with lumps of putty to keep the water out; a length of tube cut from their dad's garden hose; and a home-made hand-spear to hunt down dinner, these early diving pioneers took themselves off to the ocean in search of adventure.

Not content with the idea of merely observing the undersea

world from the shallows – and valuing the freedom of the spear fishing snorkeller – folks like Hass and Costeau hastened the introduction of self-contained breathing apparatus. Recording their own undersea exploits in books, magazine articles and documentary films, these two were driven by that same thirst for excitement and knowledge that prompted Columbus to hop in a leaky old boat and become the first cruise operator to tour the Caribbean; or Sir Edmund Hillary to go clambering up to the top of mount Everest, "because it's there." Feats that, in their day, won all of them world acclaim for their vision and courage.

Sadly times have now changed and adventure activities like diving have fallen victim to their own popularity.

Despite, (or because of?) the fact that tens of millions of people world-wide have been seduced by the idea of seeing for themselves what lies beneath the ocean's surface, recreational diving is now coming under the spotlight as an activity that governments believe they must control and regulate in order to protect people from themselves.

Nobody doubts that safety is – or should be - of paramount concern when taking part in *any* activity. But attempting to cocoon people from taking self-imposed risks is – *providing that nobody else is put in harm's way in the process* – to deny that basic urge to 'boldly go where no person has gone before', a motive that the worldwide army of non-diving bureaucrats and plaintiff lawyers don't appear to recognise.

. . .

In that regard it's interesting to consider just how far recreational diving might have come if, during Gilpatric's day, government officials had taken an interest in his early spear fishing activities.

"'Hello, lad! And just where do you think you're going dressed up like that?"

"Who are you?"

"I'm with MUM, (the Ministry of Underwater Management), and I'm investigating an anonymous tip-off that a group of people along this stretch of the coast are engaged in dangerous and potentially risky activities. What's your name?"

"I'm Guy Gilpatric. I was going for a swim in the hope of catching a fish for dinner."

"Oh, really? You'd better let me have a close look at that equipment, then. What are these? Old motorcycle goggles daubed with putty. That'll cause severe rashes and skin irritations. And see this tube, that's just a piece of garden-hose. Not at all hygienic putting that into your mouth, is it? As for these lumps of lead strung onto a piece of cord! Hasn't anyone ever told you about lead poisoning?

. . .

"They were just to help me dive down less effortlessly."

"What on earth for? You're not a fish, lad. Fish breathe in water, people can't. It's as simple as that. And talking of fish, what are you doing with this lethal looking spear? It looks to me as though I arrived in the nick of time: Swimming around unaccompanied in the open ocean; polluting the water with toxic materials; in possession of an offensive weapon; hunting fish without a licence; and publishing irresponsible material that might inspire others to put their lives at risk. They'll probably lock you up and throw away the key. It's just as well that people can rely on MUM to know what's best for them!"

Gilpatric was right! If I were you, I'd get myself off diving while the getting's good.

CHAPTER 19
VE HAF VAYS OF MAKING YOU TOCK

In 1960 a diving watch, engineered from a single block of steel and featuring a large, hemi-spherical, crystal lens, was attached to the external hull of the bathyscaphe 'Trieste'. Crewed by Jacques Piccard and Lieutenant Don Walsh, of the U.S. Navy, the 'Trieste' descended 35,800 feet to the bottom of the Marianas Trench - the deepest recorded ocean depth - and remained there for some twenty minutes before ascending back to the surface.

The watch, now on display in London's Science Museum, remained unaffected by the seventy tons or so of pressure to which it had been subjected and still worked perfectly. As a tribute to the watchmaker's art it had proven itself beyond all doubt. But as a functional timepiece it was far too bulky to be discretely hidden beneath the sleeve of a shirt or jacket.

Not that divers ever try to hide their watches. Apart from being a necessary tool-of-the-trade, they're expensive status symbols that mark the wearer as somebody worth talking to at social gatherings.

I stumbled across this dubious piece of wisdom at an early age when trying to further my acquaintance with a girl that I'd just met at a party. *Me*: "Hello! What do you do?" *She*: "I'm an Art critic. Have you seen the Surrealist exhibition at the National Gallery?" *Me*: "No! I'm a Diver." *She*: "Really? Judging by your watch, you're not a very good one! Excuse me. There's somebody over there that I really must talk to."

(Apparently my wristwatch, showing Mickey Mouse dressed in red shorts and yellow joggers semaphoring the time with his arms, was no match for those divers fortunate enough to own a 'real' diving watch. *He:* - looking at his high-priced chronometer - "Is that the time?" *She:* "Oh! You're obviously a diver. I know that they have to get to bed early. Shall we leave?")

Unable to afford one of the expensive and proven brands, I bought my first diving watch through a newspaper mail order advertisement. The Russian-made, stainless steel watch looked perfect. Best of all, it was cheap! Although supposedly water resistant to a depth of 50 metres, it only worked when it was placed face down on a flat surface. (I made this discovery on waking one morning beneath a glass-topped coffee table. From which position I was able to observe the second hand of my watch – that somehow had wound up face down on top of the said coffee table - whisk around the dial.) At any other angle the hands jammed together.

Two years later – somewhere south of Suez and still naïve in the ways of the world – I struck a deal with a street-trader for a slightly more expensive model. Depth rated to 100-metres, (I liked the idea of a 90-metre safety margin!), the watch worked perfectly up until the moment when, a few hours later, the ship sailed and I took a shower. The inside lens immediately fogged up with water droplets and the winder dropped off!

Before there's a rush to try and sell me shares in a dental care scheme for gummy sharks, the purpose in mentioning my gullible attitude is two-fold.

The first - that diving safety doesn't come with a price-tag attached!

And the second - that although diving watches are no longer the expensive equipment items that they once were, many people now dispense completely with their use in favour of a digital timer or dive computer.

Which is fine for those who own their own computers, but more problematic for divers who rely on renting equipment – particularly when travelling - and who assume the widespread availability of these instruments: Something that's not always the case.

Thanks to advances in manufacturing technology, (and with models and prices to suit all pockets and diving needs), owning a diving watch is an investment in peace of mind – even if it is only regarded as providing back-up redundancy to a dive computer.

But best of all, it symbolises the fact that the wearer is a person worth talking to at social functions!

Nowadays, when there's a strong possibility that I'll meet somebody that I want to impress, I can turn back the clock to another era.

She: "What time is it?"

Me: [Making a grand production of looking at my watch]. "It's almost ten minutes past ……".

She: "Oh! Mickey Mouse wearing a diving helmet. You're obviously a new-age, sensitive Diver. I know that they have to get to bed early. Shall we leave? ".

CHAPTER 20
THINK OR THWIM

An abstract concept that most divers claim to practice but one that they seldom think about in any depth, the phrase 'diving safety' is a classic example of an oxymoron. (For the benefit of those who believe that an oxymoron is an overweight diver festooned with cylinders who insists on making deep, deep air dives, it's actually a figure of speech in which the terms seemingly contradict one another.)

For many people safety is never an issue. Taught to believe that diving is, "fun, enjoyable – and safe", they depend on Dive-Masters and Instructors to take charge of every aspect of their dive, including assembling the equipment and acting as an underwater guide and protector. For people who think this way, diving is no more dangerous than hopping into a taxicab and hoping that the driver's sober and knows where he's going.

Although it's fair to say that the majority of recreational divers in supervisory positions welcome this responsibility, they often adopt a too protective attitude. Rather than stressing that the decision to dive should be an individual one based on ability and knowledge of the potential risks, (and that ultimately everyone must accept responsibility for their own well-being), there's a tendency to cocoon those with less-experience from diving's dark realities.

While some folks might regard such seemingly conscientious behaviour as admirable, the downside is that rather than persuading the novice to take diving seriously, it only encourages them to ignore the basic principles of safety learned during training.

Even worse, it gives rise to the belief that not only is it OK to have somebody with apparently more experience think and make decisions on another person's behalf; but that safe diving practice is somehow a measure of how long a person's been actively engaged in diving rather than what they've learned.

Often overlooked in all of this is the fact that while experience may be a good teacher, it's usually preceded by poor judgement! (Those who manage to survive poor decisions usually describe the incident as 'bad luck', but as anyone who's given any thought to the matter knows, 'luck' has even less relevance to diving safety than advice like, 'Always keep the number of ascents that you've made equal to the number of descents.')

Encouraging people to think about diving for themselves isn't dangerous; it only becomes so when those same divers 'think' that they've arrived at ironclad solutions to safety.

In a recent survey conducted by a diving magazine, divers were invited to comment on the buddy system and what – in their opinion – constituted a good buddy. Strangely enough, the novice divers gave answers like: "Somebody who shares similar underwater interests to my own." "A person who sticks to our agreed dive plan." "Someone capable of providing assistance in an emergency." And, "a person who modifies their dive to suit the speed and ability of the least experienced member of the pair."

The experienced divers, on the other hand, gave answers like: "A good buddy is somebody who doesn't worry if we become separated and they can't find me." "Someone who can keep up with me." "A person who owns a better underwater light than me." And, "it's safer to dive solo than having to worry about somebody else!"

A few even maintained that equipment configuration was the sole criteria for selecting a buddy, (a thought process remarkably similar to that of some standard-dressed divers of sixty or more years ago who argued that anyone wearing a helmet that attached to the corselet with anything less than twelve-bolts was unsafe.)

Although to be fair to this latter group, the system's leading advocates are extremely accomplished divers who practice a holistic approach to safety. They manage this by taking into consideration every aspect of the dive, including equipment configuration, training, physical fitness and mental attitude: an approach that's often opposed by those who claim that it's far too rigorous to apply to normal recreational diving.

As a complex activity, diving may never be completely safe. But with only a little thought it can be made safer. Just remember, never let your dive gear, your buddy – or anyone else – take you somewhere that your brain didn't get to at least half-an-hour earlier!

CHAPTER 21
WHITHER GOEST THOU?

Some people are blessed with the gift of always knowing exactly where they are in relation to anywhere else. Like migrating birds they have the uncanny ability to find their way from point A to point B without the need to study a map or ask for directions. Even underwater and in poor visibility they rarely need to consult their compass before navigating a direct course back to the boat or exit point.

Such people make great dive buddies. Regrettably it's not a talent that's easily acquired. For most of us, successful underwater navigation depends upon constant practice and our skill in following a compass heading; the ability to gauge the strength and direction of any currents; how well we can remember features of the underwater seascape - and even what the hull of the dive boat looks like when viewed from beneath the surface!

I'd never given much thought to this aspect of underwater navigation when diving from a vessel. Granted, I may not always have surfaced exactly back at the boat; but by guess and by God, (and always allowing my dive buddy to take the lead – and all of the blame – when I have been off course) I've usually managed to avoid the stigma of being branded as an incompetent navigator. Until recently, that is.

It was the first dive of a four-day liveaboard trip aboard *TAKA II* to dive the Ribbon Reefs that lie north of Cairns, on the outer edge of Australia's Great Barrier Reef. Arriving at the 'Cod Hole' in the early morning and anxious to get into the water, my buddy and I paid little attention to another Cairns vessel moored some 350 metres away.

"Follow me, Huw." I cried as I leaped from the boat's side. "I know this site like the back of my hand!" Huw Porter, then on holiday from the UK and who had never dived the Great Barrier Reef previously, seemed happy with the arrangement.

In warm, tropical waters with visibility at 30-plus metres, we swooped through gullies and swam between coral heads among clouds of purple and gold reef fish, damsels, angelfish, parrotfish, whitetip reef sharks and the giant potato cod after which the site is named.

Drifting across the tops of shallow corals towards the end of the dive, I saw a boat's ladder above me. Attracting Huw's attention, I tapped my watch, pointed to the hull above our heads and indicated that we should ascend. He urgently scissored his hands in front of him in a, 'no' signal. Grasping the bottom rung of the ladder and removing my fins, I again indicated that he should ascend. He shrugged in resignation, made his way to the ladder and surfaced just in time to hear an amused crewman lean towards me saying, "You're on the wrong boat, mate!"

Mumbling obscenities and blushing furiously as I put my fins back on, I looked towards *TAKA*. Nobody appeared to be pointing in our direction. "We'll swim back on the surface", I whispered to Huw, "and just tell folks onboard that we finished our dive and surfaced in this general vicinity."

It was a good face-saving plan. And we could have got away with it if the skipper of this other vessel – an old acquaintance - hadn't chosen that precise moment to look over the stern and recognise me! "Bless my soul, Strikey! Trying to jump ship again, eh?"

Some people rise to a challenge. Huw proved such a person. "We've just carried out a below-the-water-line inspection on your hull and everything appears to be OK. Will you be paying by cash or cheque?"

The splashing of our fins as we pounded our way back to TAKA drowned out the skipper's cheery farewell.

"Well Huw." I said later. "I hope my little charade proved helpful in demonstrating the importance of good underwater navigation techniques. Understanding tides and currents and how to use the compass properly are fine, but a good diver should also be able to rely on natural aids to navigation like sand-ripples, light shadows, and the effect of tidal flow on kelps and seaweeds. As I did on that last dive."

"I guessed that when – knowing that *TAKA*'s a single prop mono-hull – I saw you about to board that twin-prop catamaran." He said with a straight face.

"Right! Well now that you've seen how it's done, I'm going to let you navigate on all of the other dives. Just remember: Practice makes perfect"

CHAPTER 22
NO FEAR!

I've always held the word 'No' in high regard. Apart from its structural simplicity it's always stood by me like a good friend when I've considered myself at risk in the face of questions like, *"Was it you who put live frogs in the lavatory bowl?"* or, *"Would you care for a second helping of boiled broccoli and burned liver?"*

But despite this status as the most important term that folks can ever learn as far as their personal safety is concerned, a simple 'No!' often appears to be the most feared and least used word in diving.

Which is rather strange considering how much easier it is to remember and understand than many of the terms, formulas and technical definitions that pad out the glossaries of diving manuals.

Knowing the proper terminology is, of course, a handy asset for everyone who takes diving seriously. However, it's even more important to understand the practical significance of a term and its relevance to safe diving practice, in much the same way that it's sometimes just as useful to recognise *who* is saying something rather than *what* it is that they're saying.

Diving purists, for example, refer to flippers as 'fins', while grizzled old divers are still regarded as experienced veterans for insisting on calling their fins 'flippers'. The point being that what is said is of far less importance than understanding what is meant!

For some divers, however, 'talking the talk' has become an obsession; one that blinds them to the fact that diving is a practical activity made safer and more enjoyable when it's combined with a common sense approach to the use of language. Especially when a misunderstanding over what was said – as opposed to what was meant – could have disastrous consequences.

It wouldn't, for instance, be sensible for a Dive Master to introduce the Gas Law formulas into a dive briefing and say something like, "*On your descent keep in mind that P_1 over P_2 times V_1 equals V_2*", when all that was required was a reminder about the need to monitor gauges more often at depth.

Acronyms can be equally confusing. Diving has lots of them. AAS's; ABT's; AGE's; ATM's; ATA's; BCD's; BT's; CNS'S; DCS's, and on through the entire alphabet. Reducing names and phrases down to their initials may be a convenient form of verbal shorthand, but they're only practical when all parties in a conversation know precisely what they mean in the context in which they're used.

And further muddying the waters of intelligent and meaningful communication, diving's also blessed with its own fair share of slang expressions.

Despite these apparent obstacles, most divers quickly become familiar with the commonplace terms and expressions in regular use. A few even claim to understand what they mean!

Sadly, however, it's a learning process in which it's easy to forget the importance of simple language and the value of phrases like, "I don't know", or, "I don't understand" - and even the difference between "Yes" and "No".

"So when I asked, at the end of the dive briefing, 'Does everybody feel confident about doing this dive?' and you answered with 'Yes', what you actually meant to say was 'No'?"

"Yes! But only 'cause I was confused by all of those acro-thingies and I was too embarrassed to admit that I don't know my AAS from my elbow."

"And then when I asked - just before you and your buddy entered the water - 'Do you both understand the time, depth and air supply parameters of this dive?' and you said 'Yes', you really meant to say, 'No'? "

"No. I meant 'Yes' because my buddy seemed to understand what you said. I didn't know that he'd said 'Yes' because I hadn't said 'No'."

Fearing ridicule if they admit to ignorance or voice doubts and concerns about their ability to carry out a particular dive, there's a tendency among many divers – at every level of experience - to put pride before their personal well-being and enjoyment. Caving in to peer pressure they'll ignore all of their instincts and say 'Yes', even when their gut feeling tells them to say 'No'.

Which is just about as silly as me saying, 'Yes' when asked: *"Was it you who put live frogs in the lavatory bowl?"*

CHAPTER 23
HEROES AND VILLAINS

As somebody once pointed out, heroes are just ordinary people who do extra-ordinary things. That might well be the case. But in an activity like diving, (where nothing should ever be taken for granted), it's important to choose role models wisely. Either that or have a good back-up plan to explain away any apparent shortcomings in terms of personal courage and ability.

In my case it's easy! Faced with the prospect of either throwing my body from the back of a dive boat into high seas and a crashing swell, or staying dry and snug in a sheltered corner of the deck while taking charge of the hot coffee and biscuits, I simply tell people that without cowards like me there'd be no yardstick for measuring the deeds of the brave!

It's a great plan if you happen to believe, as I do, that it's safer and more comfortable to have heroes than to ever want to become one. Not that I lack courage. I've already proven the sort of stuff that I'm made of when, without even a thought for my own safety, I once sneaked up on a sea anemone and shot off a whole roll of film of my buddy being savaged by an angry clownfish. I've even, knowingly, entered the confines of a short swim-through just to witness nudibranchs in a feeding frenzy.

Some people reckon that I was foolhardy rather than courageous, but it does help to highlight the fact that the qualities we should look for in a diving role model need to extend beyond mere bravado.

The diving Hall of Fame is filled with such people. Not only have they pushed back the boundaries of knowledge by diving deeper, further and for longer than the rest of us, but their accomplishments usually have a greater purpose than that of demonstrating their fearlessness.

Many of them aren't even 'heroes' in the strict sense of the term. (Most would cringe at the thought that anyone could ever regard them as such.) Rather than blindly putting themselves in harm's way, they give considerable thought to their diving practices and reduce any risks to an acceptable and manageable level before setting out to achieve their goals.

Although truly worthy of our respect, people like these face a lot of competition from other diving leaders who push themselves and their followers beyond the limits of good sense.

Afraid that their admirers will think less of them if they admit to doubt and uncertainty, these people exercise a dark influence over diving by encouraging unnecessary risk taking, a vicious cycle in which it often becomes difficult to tell a deserving hero from a reluctant villain.

The problem is, of course, that none of us like to think of heroes as just ordinary people who occasionally like to kick back with a beer and a pizza; who have interests outside of diving; and who have to change their underwear as frequently as the rest of us!

It's one of the reasons that so many people hold comic-book superheroes like 'Aquaman' in such high regard. As Protector of the Oceans, he was the kipper's slippers! Not only could he breathe underwater and withstand the pressure of enormous depths, but he could also communicate telepathically with all forms of marine life and swim at speeds of up to 100 miles per hour. (Something that obviously requires a streamlined body and that helps explain why, unlike so many other superheroes, he finally elected to wear his underpants beneath his trousers!)

Mind you, just having fantastic powers didn't always imply that the possessor would only use them to do good. For every superhero, there was always a super-villain swimming around desperately trying to persuade guppies to turn on Aquaman and rip him to shreds.

Tactics that sometimes parallel those of the real world of diving where many prominent divers, (people whose achievements we might otherwise have admired), succumb to the pressure of fame and die needlessly while attempting to live up to the expectations of those who hold them in high regard.

Which points up the fact that ordinary people aren't cut out to be heroes. It takes a lot of courage – and a firm belief in the old saying, *"There are old divers; there are bold divers: But there ain't no old, bold divers!"*

CHAPTER 24
LAYING DOWN THE LAW

As a practical activity almost every aspect of diving can be reduced to a handful of basic scientific laws and principles that govern our safe enjoyment. We may not be familiar with the formulas, but the chances are that everybody who dives understands that, for example, Boyles Law relates to volume/pressure relationships and the dangers of holding one's breath on ascent; that Dalton's Law of Partial Pressures defines how deep we can go breathing a particular mix of gas; and that Archimedes Principle governs how much weight is required to achieve neutral buoyancy when wearing a thick wet-suit.

As divers, it's important to know these things, and the very reason that so much emphasis is placed on them. Equally significant, however, but far less well understood, are the many other 'Laws' and 'Rules' that apply to diving but that are often overlooked, or ignored altogether.

. . .

Take, for example, all of the major contributions to diving made by Sir Isaac Newton during the seventeenth century. There he was sitting under an apple tree when a 'Golden Delicious' dropped from the branch above him and landed on his head. "Gadzooks!" He probably exclaimed, (people in the 17th century were fond of saying things like "Gadzooks"); and then, after a moment's pause, "Bless my soul. I've just discovered Gravity!" (A breakthrough in scientific thinking that, even today, isn't well understood by some divers who, regardless of the sensitivity of toes, insist on tossing weight-belts around in the confines of a cramped dive boat!)

Flushed with success at his ability to explain in scientific terms why it was that apples fell to the ground rather than drifting upwards into outer space, Newton turned his attention to other naturally occurring phenomena and began to formulate lots of other Laws that have relevance to diving.

Things like: *'For every action there must be an equal and opposite reaction'*, a Law that's regularly misinterpreted by careless divers who still haven't come to terms with the fact that the 'opposite reaction' to dropping a weight belt onto somebody's toes is more likely to be a torrent of abuse, followed by a judicious whack around the side of the head, than by a grateful, "Thank you!"

Although it doesn't have the force of Law to back it up, it does seem to me that a blow to the head, (whether caused by an apple or an injured diver's fist), may be what some people require in order to stimulate their thought processes.

. . .

At the very least it may cause them to begin viewing diving as the discipline that it is and rid them of the notion that scientific laws formulated several hundred years ago have somehow exceeded their 'use-by' date, or that the proven common sense 'Rules' of diving are more than just minor obstacles to be overcome.

Consider, for example, the 'buddy system', an established practical technique that, for decades, has been regarded as one of the cornerstones of safe and enjoyable recreational diving experiences. And then consider the article, promoting the launch of a solo diving specialty course published in a major diving magazine headlined, *"Why the Buddy System is dangerous."*

"All right, you 'orrible little lot, the purpose of this course is to teach you the advantages of self-sufficiency and diving alone. (And looking around, I can immediately see – judging by your physical appearance – that many of you have no other option!).

"Because – as solo divers - there'll be nobody with whom to share the experience or to call upon for advice or assistance, there will be no instructors present with you while you perform the required in-water skills. Instead, we'll be relying on the 'honour' system and assessing your competence on whether you manage to navigate back to the exit point successfully.

. . .

"As for the rest of it ... well! There's not a lot too it, really. Just make sure that you've paid your money so that I can then issue you with a certification card allowing you to dive by yourself anywhere, anytime you wish."

There may well be a case for teaching self-sufficiency and solo-diving, but to promote it by denigrating the proven and reliable buddy system is about as absurd as suggesting that falling apples might go drifting off into outer space.

CHAPTER 25
GETTING THE THIRD DEGREE

The problem with leaving my radio-alarm volume turned down to a gentle, background drone is that while I'm slowly waking up to another day, I often confuse the tail end of dreams with news reports. (I once mistook a dream about whales with the live radio coverage of a Welsh rugby union game and spent an entire week convinced that Humpback whales were cruising the oceans of the world singing 'Men of Harlech'!

On another occasion, and still half-asleep, I thought that the finance reporter was advising people to sell all of their socks. Fortunately for my comfort – if not my pride – a stockbroker friend explained that there wasn't actually much of a market for used socks emblazoned with cartoon characters!) Which is why, when I recently awoke to a news report that several universities in different parts of the world were offering degree courses in surfing, I dismissed the idea as being just another sleep-induced delusion.

. . .

Apparently, however, it's true! Folks who want to advance their knowledge of surfing can now undertake a University course in the subject and receive, after completing several years of formal study, a Degree entitling them to put letters after their name. What's even stranger is the fact that they don't even have to know how to surf to be accepted into the programme!

Leaving to one side any bias on my part, it struck me as odd that surfing - an activity based solely on a person's ability to stand upright on a wooden plank while coasting along on the top of a wave - should be considered worthy of scholarly pursuit; especially when diving – encompassing disciplines like physics, physiology, chemistry, biology, engineering, mechanics, electronics, history, film-making, environmentalism and the like – is left out in the academic cold.

The underlying reason for this apparent anomaly is, of course, obvious. A Degree course in diving would not be in the best interests of either the global economy; universities and other tertiary places of learning; or of the diving industry itself.

Rather than enrolling in Economics, Urban Planning, Social Sciences, or Law, the student demand for diving would undoubtedly see a decline in such subjects and the eventual closing of those university departments. Governments would be obliged to function with smaller bureaucracies; taxes would be lowered; there would be fewer traffic lights and confusing one-way street systems in our cities; 'political correctness' would be given the old heave-ho; and lawyers wouldn't feel the need to chase ambulances in order to earn a living. It'd be the end of civilisation, as we know it!

A good thing too, I hear some of you say, but consider the effect that it might have on diving:

"So. You want to do your post-graduate studies aboard my dive boat, eh?"

"Yes, please, Instructor Professor."

"Got your framed parchment degree with you, I see. Ah! An honours graduate from the University of Krakatoa, eh? One of Hermione Catfolly's students, I suppose? Still putting the emphasis on Gas Laws, is she?"

"Yes. Actually, she's a bit of a stickler when it comes to things like Charles's Law."

"Is she now? So if I fill a SCUBA tank with air at 16.7 ATM's, at 24°C, but then leave it out in the sun to warm to 65°C., what will the tank pressure increase to?"

"Errmm! Uhm! Err! 20.5 atmospheres?"

. . .

"Balderdash! It's 19.0 ATM's, a simple problem that any under-graduate diver could solve! Don't believe me, eh? Go and ask, Krabbman over there. He's already earned a Doctorate in Dive-Mastering with his controversial thesis on the molecular properties of wet-suit neoprene and, in the process, become an indispensable member of this dive boat's crew.

"Nevertheless – after four years of study – you're obviously anxious to put some of the theory that you've learned into practice, so today we'll start you off with the basics of snorkelling and then, after a month or two, decide if you're ready for SCUBA. How's that sound?"

"But, Professor, I thought that once I'd mastered the theory and earned my degree that I'd be qualified to actually dive?"

"You're under a grave misapprehension, Lad. We're not dilettantes. We're serious academics. If you expect to be taken seriously in diving, then you'll do it our way or not at all."

Come to think of it, there's really no need for a formal Degree when some sectors of the diving community are already convinced that their approach to diving is, geometrically-speaking, the only right angle!

CHAPTER 26
A CHAIN REACTION

There are distinct advantages in being at the top of the food chain. One of the most obvious being the fact that hamburgers and pizza are higher up the scale than broccoli! It's a system that's worked well and one that we've managed to refine by successfully relegating most of the competition (other land-based predators) to a lower rung on the ladder.

Taming the world's oceans has been far more difficult. Especially where sharks are concerned. Evolving into perfect feeding machines over the course of 425 million years, sharks have managed to acquire a reputation that owes more to fiction than to fact; one that's become tainted by movies like *"Jaws"*, and books with graphic cover blurbs like: *"Its grim savagery is horrifying but you will be compelled to remember the dreaded scavenger hungry for human flesh."* (From a book first published in 1959.)

It's a view of sharks that's held sway ever since the first caveman toddled off down to the beach for a bit of a paddle and had his toes mistaken for sardines: An honest enough blunder in poor visibility, but one that continues to be exploited by ill-informed alarmists who maintain that, in the kill-or-be-killed world of their imagination, it's in humanity's best interest to exterminate all sharks.

In that regard – and demonstrating a savagery that makes any shark look like a spineless jellyfish by comparison - the score has definitely been in man's favour. Each year tens of millions of sharks are fished from the ocean for food or as sport. In many instances the fins, prized as a delicacy in some parts of the world, are cruelly sliced from the beasts and their still living bodies thrown back into the water to die and be eaten by their fellows.

Even recreational divers were once caught up in the hysteria. Armed with spear guns and power-heads it became commonplace during the 'sixties and 'seventies for divers to slaughter sharks in their hundreds. On the eastern seaboard of Australia alone, whole colonies of the Grey Nurse shark, (a fish-eating species falsely reputed to be a 'man-killer'), were hunted almost to the point of extinction.

To their credit, a majority of today's recreational divers have since become leading marine conservationists. Swapping spear guns for cameras, they've been instrumental in showing us that the only thing we need to fear in the oceans is our own ignorance.

That's not to suggest that sharks aren't dangerous. Many of them are, as witnessed by the wide publicity given to a spate of shark attacks on swimmers in the waters off of Florida a few years ago. Separate tragedies that saw the State's Fish and Wildlife Conservation Commission (FWC) overturn dive industry guidelines on inter-action with the marine environment and impose a complete ban on shark diving and the feeding of marine life.

A decision that, paradoxically, received the support of spear fishing groups as well as self-styled 'environmentalists', with both factions implying that dive operators conducting organised shark feeds in remote areas were ecological vandals whose practices threatened public safety.

In keeping with that piece of absurdity, the ban fell short of including commercial fishermen using blood and offal to attract sharks; anglers dangling lines with live bait impaled on a hook; or to spear fishermen who – in the wake of the attacks – wantonly slaughtered and beheaded colonies of nurse sharks: Acts that went unremarked by the 'environmentalists'.

Just to put shark attacks into perspective, in 1999 there were 58 confirmed attacks worldwide with a total of four fatalities. Meanwhile, in the USA alone, road deaths for that same year numbered 41,345.

It's often suggested that bee stings, snake and spider bites and being hit by lightning all exact a greater toll than sharks. Which might well be true, but they're still in the junior league when compared with humans.

During 1987, in New York City, 1,587 people received treatment after being bitten by another human whereas, in the whole of the USA, just 13 injuries were attributed to shark attacks.

And in 1996 when 18 shark attacks were recorded across the USA, 43,687 New Yorkers were obliged to seek medical treatment for injuries sustained while seated on the toilet bowl! (Whoever compiled that piece of information didn't see fit to specify the nature of the injuries, or exactly how they occurred. Krabbmann suggested that there might be some truth to the urban myth about hungry alligators living in the sewers beneath the city!)

And then there's cancer. A disease that each year accounts for more fatalities than the combined number of shark attacks throughout the whole of human history. And one that, according to some researchers, may ultimately be defeated through a better understanding of what it is that makes sharks tick.

All things considered, sharks have received a bum rap from humans. It's a situation that's not helped by turning back the clock and – by resurrecting old myths and fears about them – attempting to eradicate them. That's about as intelligent as suggesting that we get rid of automobiles and toilet bowls!

After all, putting the bite on sharks may ultimately be bad for our health!

CHAPTER 27
TALK'S CHEAP. TECHNOLOGY ISN'T

Ted Turner, the founder of CNN, once claimed during an interview that he owed his success to his father who had advised him to, "never set yourself goals that you *can* achieve!"

An inspirational piece of advice that, (despite sounding as though it fell out of a fortune cookie), set the scene for CNN's explosive growth into a global news and communications' empire.

Lacking CNN's financial and technical resources, our own modest efforts to establish a viable underwater communications system hit an enormous stumbling block during a recent charter-boat expedition to film a documentary on exotic marine life.

Before we'd even cast off from the wharf, we knew that the expedition was doomed. Finding a small packet of fortune cookies hidden away in the galley, Krabbmann sneaked out on deck and began stuffing them into his mouth until a coughing fit alerted us to his distress.

"Pthweehh!" he said, blowing crumbs and half-chewed pieces

of paper over the side. "These aren't biscuits, they're death traps for the unwary!" He threw the remaining two cookies over the stern and straight into the beak of a circling albatross that – after struggling to swallow the things – crashed onto the deck.

"That doesn't bode well for the trip." Said Tricky, the dive supervisor, who immediately tried to dislodge the offending cookie trapped in the bird's gullet. "Haven't any of you read, "The Rhyme of the Ancient Mariner", about all the ill-luck that befell the ship after he killed an albatross? There! That's better!" The relieved albatross struggled to the side of the vessel and soared away, leaving Tricky holding a small fragment of paper that simply said, 'Never set yourself goals ...'!

All of that was forgotten in the trip out to the reef. The sea was calm, the weather perfect, and all of the equipment that we'd be using, (including the underwater communications gear and topside video relay), had been double-checked and functioned perfectly. Until it came time to dive.

"There's a large cowrie shell with the mantle slowly opening in the bottom of the picture." Said Krabbmann, monitoring the video from the deck of the vessel. "Just zoom in on it."

"Wh ... (squawk, squelch) ... ay? (Crackle)... ease ...(spluurk) eat it!"

"Eat it? No you can't eat it. I repeat. I want you to film it in close-up." Krabbmann replied.

"What don't you want me ... (phlllt) ... o eat?"

"I didn't tell you to eat anything!" Roared an increasingly frustrated Krabbmann. "I just wanted you to ... Hello! Hello! Can you hear me?"

The unit had died. Whatever the initial cause, it was a condition that Tricky pronounced as terminal after viewing the results of Krabbmann's attempts at resuscitation using a large hammer.

"Now how do I tell them what I want them to film?" Bemoaned Krabbmann, looking at the video monitor. Tricky offered a solution.

"I suppose we could always attach a signal line to the camera-man and then – using a pre-arranged system of simple 'Pulls and Bells' similar to those that the old standard divers used to use – you could direct them left, right, up, down, zoom in, zoom out."

The diving camera-man was briefed and – after an accelerated programme in which he and Krabbmann practiced sending and receiving line signals – he descended back to his chosen spot by the reef wall.

Poised in front of the video monitor and tightly grasping the line, Krabbmann watched the screen closely. "There!" He suddenly yelled, jumping up and pointing to the monitor. "A fire clam! A fire cl ..." The screen dissolved into a flurry of bubbles as the diver was jerked away from the reef.

"We can always try sound signals." Said the ever-inventive Tricky. "You seem happy with a hammer. Using the same code as for the line signals, just tap on the ladder. The sound, being magnified and conducted more easily through the denser medium of water, will let the diver know what you want."

Nobody expressed surprise when, on Krabbmann's first attempt to communicate his wishes to the diver by tapping on the ship's ladder, it suddenly disappeared over the side, to reappear a moment later on the video monitor as an image crashing onto the reef below.

Lips tight set, Tricky emerged from the galley with two

empty tin cans and a ball of string. Punching a hole in the base of each can, he connected the two together and handed it to Krabbmann.

"Do you think it'll work?" Krabbmann asked.

Tricky responded with a time-honoured hand signal that, for such a simple, two-fingered gesture, communicated volumes and served to highlight the fact that – regardless of language barriers and without need of words – divers really can be excellent communicators!

CHAPTER 28
I WISH I'D SAID THAT

Sometimes it's easy to forget that diving's meant to be fun and something to be enjoyed. Particularly when you find yourself trapped in the confines of a small dive boat with a group of people who attract misfortune, and who then attempt to explain it all away with nuggets of folk-wisdom drawn from a seemingly inexhaustible supply of proverbs and clichés.

"I'm sorry about that", said Krabbmann, quickly removing his size twelve boot from the shattered remains of my facemask, "but it's no use crying over spilt milk. Accidents will happen!" At that moment the heavy weight belt that he'd been nervously swinging backwards and forwards hit the Dive-Master on the shin.

Doubling over in agony and thrown off balance by the motion of the boat, the divemaster toppled forward, his outstretched hand clutching for anything that would prevent his fall. He might have succeeded had Tim and his buddy not been midway through a backward roll entry over the boat's side. Receiving a clip on the jaw from a heavy-duty fin, the divemaster staggered backwards, snagged Tim's primary air hose in his hand and tumbled to the deck with a hose and regulator – minus the mouthpiece - clutched firmly in his grasp.

"Bad luck always comes in threes." Said the stoic, Krabbmann, tossing his weight-belt to one side and oblivious of the fact that it had landed in the lap of a seated diver trying to tend to the semi-conscious divemaster.

Stepping across the bodies of the purple-faced diver gasping for air and that of the groaning divemaster, Krabbmann peered over the side of the boat. "If anything can go wrong, it will." He said, philosophically.

Rescued by the quick actions of his dive buddy from the froth of bubbles that had surrounded him, Tim was assisted back on board, coughing and spluttering from the seawater that he'd inhaled while trying to breathe through the redundant mouthpiece still clamped between his teeth. Angrily discarding his cylinder – and unaware that nobody had hold of it – it crashed onto one of the outboard engines wrenching free the fuel hose.

With fuel spraying across the deck and over the equipment, the skipper rushed to fix the problem.

"Never mind." Said Krabbmann. "Worse things happen at sea!"

"We are at sea." Pointed out Tim, sadly surveying the remains of his ruined equipment. "What's even worse, we're all in the same boat!"

Ignoring this implied criticism, Krabbmann's optimism went into overdrive. "Come tomorrow, we'll all look back on this and laugh about it. Anyway. All's well that ends well!"

As the boat limped back to shore, I couldn't help but wonder why there was no silver lining in the black cloud hanging over us all? And then, why it is that we rely so much on clichés to explain away our mistakes and inadequacies?

Diving has plenty of such commonplace sayings in daily use – which people seldom think too deeply about. *'Diving is Safe, Fun, and Enjoyable'*, springs instantly to mind. It's a short sentence based on long experience of what works and what doesn't, but it's one that many divers believe to be unquestionably true.

Recreational diving certainly should be 'fun' and it should be 'enjoyable'. But it's certainly not 'safe' unless people are first properly trained in the type of diving that they want to do, and are subsequently prepared to temper that training with common sense and a lot of thought.

Which leads to another diving cliché - *'Know your limitations, and dive within them!'* Ignoring their present level of fitness and lack of any recent experience in the type of dive being undertaken, many people believe that their certification level alone determines their limitations. In failing to differentiate between 'certified' and 'qualified' they become, *an accident waiting to happen.*

Forgetting that there are, *'Old divers and bold divers, but no old, bold divers'*, they often put themselves into harm's way by ignoring the old adage, *'Never allow yourself to get into a situation that you cannot get out of all by yourself.'*

Safe and successful diving requires more than just a mastery of technique; it also requires a lot of common sense coupled with an appreciation of the obligations that we have to our buddies as well as ourselves.

"Do unto others as you would have them do unto you." Said Krabbmann, once we were back on shore. "C'mon, I'll buy you all as much beer as you can drink while we plan the next dive. Tomorrow's another day!"

"No thanks." Replied Tim. "I don't like looking a gift horse in the mouth, but *'Today's dive starts the night before'*. Anyway, going on another dive with you would be like stepping out of the frying pan into the fire.

CHAPTER 29
HEADS AND TALES

There's no finer place for keeping abreast of all that's happening in diving than the front bar of the 'The Sozzled Cod'. As a gathering point for divers of every level of experience and underwater interest, it's a place where reputations have been made – and tarnished. Just recently a regular made the claim that he'd taught me everything that I knew about diving; until somebody else pointed out that I actually knew very little and that the boast wasn't much of a reflection on his teaching skills!

As a person still basking in the glory of having set a new world depth record, (to the best of my knowledge, nobody else has gone to the expense of using trimix for a three-metre shore dive!) I ignored the taunts. Until, that is, Krabbmann began pontificating about snorkels and I confessed to always carrying one with me. Overhearing my remark, the same person who'd cast doubts upon my diving abilities, couldn't resist the opportunity to put the boot in for a second time. "You can't be serious, Strike?" He said, loudly enough for everyone to hear, "Real divers don't carry snorkels!"

Judging by the pitying looks that I received, it was obvious that more than half of the people in the room agreed with him. "It might just be me", said Krabbmann, arching his eyebrows, "but from what I've seen lately it would certainly appear that snorkels have gone out of vogue. How many divers have you seen recently with a snorkel strapped to the left hand side of their face mask?"

It was a good point. Especially in light of the fact that an increasing number of divers are adopting a more streamlined and practical approach to equipment configuration; one in which a snorkel can become not only a general entanglement hazard, but also interferes with the smooth passing off of a long hose in an air sharing emergency.

As a system popularised by leaders of the world's foremost cave diving exploration team, the equipment platform's clean, uncluttered lines translates well to all types of diving: a process in which the snorkel, (an equipment item with no practical benefit for a diver exploring the water-filled confines of a cave tunnel) is increasingly regarded as a hindrance rather than a necessity when diving in the open ocean.

In that environment, it's always seemed to me that a snorkel's a useful tool for divers to carry. Especially when you want to conserve air, or when you face a long surface swim back to the boat or shore.

Heads, after all, are very dense and heavy things that seem naturally designed to float face down in the water with the nose acting like a yacht's keel. Constantly having to lift it up in order to breathe is hard work.

"In that case" said Krabbmann, "you simply make yourself buoyant and swim along on your back."

Which is fine for short hauls but not very practical over long distances when, in order to avoid cramping, it's usually more comfortable and convenient to be able to alternate between a face-up and a face-down position in the water.

I say this from experience, having once surfaced from a dive together with my two buddies, (we were the only passengers on the vessel) to see our dive boat disappearing over the horizon as the skipper followed an imaginary trail of bubbles towards China.

Faced with a long surface swim to the nearest island and a general unwillingness to ditch our gear, we set off swimming on our backs. Tiring of this, and not making a great deal of headway, I removed the telescopic snorkel, that I always carry in my wetsuit pocket, and began swimming face down towards land. Lacking snorkels the other two divers also assumed the face down position, breathing from their regulators until they'd exhausted the remaining gas in their cylinders. At which point they were both obliged to begin swimming on their backs.

Unable to alternate between finning styles, and slowing down as the muscle strain began to tell on them both, one developed a cramp that required me to tow him the remainder of the way to the beach and safety.

"I don't know whether either of them ever regarded themselves as 'real divers' before or since that day." I told my critic. "But rather than making blanket statements to the effect that: 'real divers don't use snorkels', (and encouraging impressionable new divers to dispense with their use completely) what you should be asking is, 'Where can I stow my snorkel so that it's not an entanglement hazard, but still available in case of need?'"

To give him his due, it was a question that he'd obviously thought deeply about. He told me exactly where I could stick my snorkel!

CHAPTER 30
FIT FOR NOTHING

As one of those people who think that a paper-cut is a major wound and who has a tendency to faint at the sight of blood, especially when it's my own, (I've said it before, but without cowards like me, there'd be no yardstick by which to measure the deeds of the brave!) I've often thought that if we were really meant to understand the inner workings of our bodies then our skin would be transparent.

It's not one of the all-time great arguments, but it does help point up the mind-set that many divers have towards all of those sloppy bits and pieces packaged up inside their skin: Providing that all of the parts stay where they're meant to be and continue to do whatever it is that they're supposed to, then who really wants to know, let alone see, what's happening to last night's beer and cheeseburger?

It's a widespread attitude and one that carries over into diving when divers overlook the need to properly understand the behaviour of breathing gases and the physiological effects of pressure on their body. Disregarding what little theory they've managed to learn about safe diving practices, they place the emphasis on equipment and ignore the importance of personal health and fitness in the equation.

Relying on the dive computer on their wrist, (rather than the one between their ears) to protect them from harm, they'll ensure that it's properly and carefully maintained and that the battery power never falls below a certain minimum level. After which - and forgetting that today's dive starts the night before with adequate sleep and rest - they'll party all night before turning up tired, hung-over and dehydrated for an early morning boat dive.

With a growing appeal across all age groups and all levels of personal ability, the standards of fitness, both physical and mental, that were once universally applied to everyone wanting to take up diving have gradually been eroded and pushed into the background by a pre-occupation with equipment and technology.

In their rush to leap into the water, it's becoming increasingly more rare to find divers who pay anything other than lip service to the pre-dive buddy-checks; and rarer still to hear those who ask the question, "Are you fit to dive?"

As a person whose former lifestyle revolved around tobacco, alcohol and late nights in *'The Sozzled Cod'* (and now somebody who proves the old adage that, 'there's none so pure as the purified') my dive buddy, Krabbmann, always manages to make the question sound like an insult.

Already on board the boat for an early morning departure, we watched a pair of obviously partied-out divers stagger down the jetty towards us, stopping briefly to stub out their cigarettes on a bollard before clambering slowly over the side of the vessel.

"Are you sure you're fit for this dive?" asked Krabbmann

"'Course, I am! I'll be fine once I'm in the water." Said the leader, taking a long swig from a bottle of fizzy soft drink and reaching into his packet for another cigarette.

"Really?" Said Krabbmann, who's been reading a lot of diving literature lately, "You know that excessive alcohol consumption will, among other things, cause dehydration that, in turn, can aggravate the onset of a 'bend'? And have ..."

"No problems there." Interrupted the leader. "I'm using a nitrox mix. The lower nitrogen content and high partial pressure of oxygen is just what the doctor ordered. I'll be right as rain and ready to party after a couple of dives."

" ... you any idea", continued Krabbmann, glaring pointedly at the unlit cigarette, "what smoking's doing to your body, let alone to the bodies of those nearby? You've probably never heard of 'free radicals', have you?"

"I have." Said the second diver. "They're a funk band."

"Are they?" Said the leader. "'Free Radicals'? Sounds more to me like one of those political slogans that blokes wearing black cloaks and big floppy hats spray-paint on alley walls. Anyway! There's no need to worry about whether I'm fit for diving. I'm an Instructor."

"I'm not pooh-poohing your theory about why skin is not transparent," said Krabbmann, turning towards me, "but in their case it wouldn't do any good. Their bodies are covered by a wet-suit and you wouldn't be able to tell whether or not they've got a brain because it's so well hidden by bone!"

CHAPTER 31
THE DIVER'S PRAYER

For all of his faults – and he has lots of them – my former dive buddy, Krabbmann, always tries to maintain a grasp on what's important in diving and what's not. Sadly, however, he usually fails to apply the things that he instinctively knows to be correct to his own diving practices. A shortcoming that, (when coupled with his, "do as I say, not as I do" attitude towards anyone whom he suspects of being less knowledgeable or experienced in diving than himself) has marked him as a Person-Who-Dives, rather than the Diver that he could be.

It's a subtle distinction; one in which people-who-dive are often mistaken for divers by virtue of their proficiency in the fundamental skills, their knowledge of the theoretical principles of diving, and because they happen to have a concertina-fold of certification cards in almost everything, from Underwater Knife Fighting through to Snorkel Maintenance.

(There are, of course, some people-who-dive who will never be mistaken for divers. Convinced that the ability to breathe through a regulator is pretty much all that's required in order to survive underwater, they manage to mask their ignorance by 'talking the talk' and pinning their faith on technology to keep them from harms way.)

Divers, on the other hand, often start out as people-who-dive until they finally wake up to the fact that a training course and certification card – of whatever level – is not an end in itself but just another rung on an endless ladder of learning; and that true experience is measured as much by what they've managed to discover about themselves as by the number of years that they've been diving. Coming to regard textbooks and manuals as useful tools rather than articles of faith, the true diver is one who, understanding his/her personal limitations, learns to temper book knowledge with a generous dollop of common sense and a lot of forethought about the activity.

Something that, despite his many years of diving, seems to have passed Krabbmann by.

A group of us had spent months searching for the scattered remains of a historical wreck that we were keen to locate. With its final resting place narrowed down to a small offshore area of seabed in 35-metres of water, we planned the dive and arranged to meet at the boat jetty bright and early on the appointed morning.

"Have any of you checked today's weather forecast?" I asked, looking at the huge slop beyond the harbour entrance and already feeling queasy.

"Those forecasters never get it right," said Krabbmann. "Anyway. It'll be OK once we get beneath the surface."

"I'm not going diving in conditions like that," I said "I've just remembered that rule about never diving with idiots - and anyone who wants to go diving in seas like those has to be an idiot."

Ignoring the criticism, Krabbmann turned to the others. "We've invested a lot of time in this search and we're not about to let a little slop and chop put us off, are we?" he asked. They all nodded agreement. "Besides which", he added, turning to me, "you've done dives in far worse conditions than this without any problems."

"That was when I was young and foolish – and being highly paid." I said. "This is recreational diving. It's supposed to be fun. Nobody's paying us to take unnecessary risks. Anyway, that wreck's been down there for eighty years and another day or two's not going to make any difference."

"If you want to wimp out because you're not up to the same standard of diving excellence as the rest of the team, then we're better off without you," said Krabbmann. "But don't expect us to share any of the glory when we come back with proof that we've found the vessel's remains."

"I think I'll stay behind", I replied, "and offer up a prayer for you all."

Krabbmann just grunted as they cast off the lines and headed towards the open sea.

Two hours later the battered group staggered back through the door of the dive shop led by a fuming and disgruntled Krabbmann. "We didn't even get into the water," he ranted. "None of them saw fit to properly secure the gear; cylinders were rolling about everywhere. Three of these so-called divers were too busy hanging over the sides and feeding the fishes to be of any use; and on top of that, the anchor snagged. The boat was bouncing around so much that we couldn't recover it. Eventually we just had to cut the line. That prayer of yours didn't help one bit."

"It's good to see you all back safely, but that prayer was for my benefit not yours," I told him.

"Eh." Said Krabbmann. "So what did you pray for?"

"It's the Diver's Prayer; a simple one that I learned many years ago from an old offshore diving supervisor." I replied. "I'll teach it to you. It goes like this: Lord protect me from amateurs and fools."

CHAPTER 32
TO 'AIR' IS HUMAN ...???

Trying to forecast where we're going is made infinitely easier when we're able to look back and see where we've been! More often than not it's a fascinating exercise in hindsight, one that manages to reveal that where we are today is not necessarily where we thought or hoped we'd be when we dreamed - a decade or more ago - of what the future might hold. Recreational diving is no exception - as I discovered while flicking through the musty pages of my hoard of old diving magazines.

Reflecting the changes that have taken place in our approach to diving over the last half-century, many of these publications have become nothing more than vague memories. With small circulations and an appeal to a hard core of pioneering enthusiasts, the editorial emphasis was very much on the DIY adventure of diving. (One of them advised readers on how to make an underwater light by linking up four 1.5-volt dry cell batteries in series with a soldering iron. "Scrounge an old torch reflector and bulb holder and attach your wires to a six volt bulb. Shove the lot into a half-pound preserving jar and pack it tight with newspaper so the reflector is pressed against the bottom of the jar. Join up the two wires before you leap over the side. A night dive is worth wasting a set of batteries anyway. Close the jar with a preserving seal and screw top lid")

Not all magazines were as in touch with the grass roots needs of divers as that one! Recently, after a fifty-one year reign as the doyen of recreational diving publications, 'Skin Diver' magazine decided to call it a day and shut up shop. Its demise met with a mixed response from the diving community. Some claimed that the publication's closure marked the end of a diving era. Others – less kindly - suggested that the magazine had, in recent years, become nothing more than a catalogue of diving destinations; one whose increasingly conservative views on diving issues directly reflected its dependency on advertising.

Whatever the truth of the matter, 'Skin Diver' magazine's enormous worldwide readership did appear to lend credibility to the opinions that it broadcast from its lofty perch. But while the new publishing kids on the block – magazines like 'aquaCORPS' – soared with the eagles, Skin Diver's slow response to the changing directions in recreational diving sometimes relegated it to scratching around on the farmyard floor.

In January 1994, its leader page critiqued an article about diving with mixed gas that had appeared in, 'Sports Illustrated' magazine – a publication with a stated readership of 23 million. The 'Skin Diver' editorial stated, in part: "I tried to rationalise that this type of diving should be considered part and parcel of recreational diving. I really made an effort to see nitrox from an experienced diver's point of view. But when all is said and done, there is no amateur application of this commercial technology. This is commercial and professional diving, pure and simple. If amateur divers want to experiment with commercial techniques, that's up to them. When they cross the line and say this is the future of recreational diving and recommend it to anyone with a Certification-card (with or without additional training), it's time to pick sides."

The article later went on to say, "Compressed air is the gas of choice for more than 99 percent of all recreational divers. Our training classes taught us to use compressed air correctly underwater to avoid personal injury. Judging by the minuscule number of bends cases, this system works – and air works!

"The proponents of nitrox and trimix seem to be willing to go to any length to sell their 'soap'. Ordinary air, they tell you, is dangerous. Narcosis is just around the corner if you use ordinary air. You're much more likely to get bent if you use ordinary air. Their use of innuendo, pseudo-science and just plain scare tactics to promote 'enriched air' is a self serving ruse even the worst used car salesman wouldn't employ."

It was a view that received considerable support at the time. I even recall a hyperbaric M.D., one who was opposed to the use of mixed gasses for recreational diving, who stated that, "we were intended to breathe air!" (He neglected to say that we were also intended to breathe air at atmospheric pressure!)

The article concluded with: "There is a very large number of diving professionals who have dedicated themselves to making diving with air as safe as possible. These professionals continue to refine safety and education techniques that allow us to dive safely using air.

"Using smoke, a tiny handful of nitrox proponents got a chance to tell 23 million people that the way 99 percent of us dive is dangerous. Please tell me that it's not the future of diving."

It was a brave stance, one that bore remarkable similarities to King Canute who, in 1016 – and convinced by his nobles that he was omnipotent – had his throne placed upon a beach and, seating himself upon it, commanded the incoming tide to retreat. It didn't and the king suffered from wet feet and a bruised ego.

Now, more than a decade after that editorial appeared in 'Skin Diver', the use of both nitrox and trimix are commonplace. There's even a growing - albeit reluctant in some quarters - acceptance of the fact that deep diving on air doesn't make you attractive to members of the opposite sex, or put hairs on your chest.

But it does make you wonder how, 'the world's best read scuba magazine' would have treated that small handful of divers who now suggest that air is far from being the best breathing medium for safe diving; and that even within the accepted recreational depth diving limits, triox, (helium enriched gas) is a far safer option!

CHAPTER 33
HOW TO SURVIVE A DIVE SHOW

Surviving the annual crop of Dive Shows and attendant Conferences takes stamina: Keeping your workload to the minimum while managing to enhance your professional reputation requires finesse!

Regular appearances at the international round of diving industry events have, for many people, become an increasingly important part of the job brief. They represent an opportunity to establish important business relationships and provide valuable links in expanding their network of contacts. A task made significantly more difficult for those delegates who believe that the business of diving is best conducted in the stuffy confines of a conference room rather than in the air-conditioned comfort of a hotel bar or coffee shop

Here, for the benefit of the uninitiated, are a few pointers to cutting-edge networking. Careful adherence to these principles will make it possible to attend – and benefit from – as many Dive Shows and conferences as the boss throws your way.

1. Carry with you, at all times, a large sheaf of documents. This will indicate to other delegates that you are:

a. Literate. (An important attribute in the diving industry!)

b. That you are either coming from a meeting/seminar session, or

c. Going to a meeting/seminar session.

2. Make a point of attending the following sessions:

a. The Opening Session. Use this session to categorise delegates into two broad areas: Competitors and Customers. Ignore the customers and concentrate on identifying the competition. These people are your enemies! Impress upon them the need to 'hard sell' prospective customers during the interval breaks and the importance of attending every session except:-

b. The 'Boring' Session. Carefully select the speaker you feel is least likely to attract a large audience. Ingratiate yourself with the Organisers by sitting in a prominent position and feigning interest in the topic.

c. The Closing Session. Concentrate on the customers. At this stage in the conference they will be shell-shocked by the attentions of your competitors. Let yours be the last and most persuasive voice that they hear.

. . .

3. Unless you are actually out diving – or otherwise enjoying yourself! – ensure that you are always visible during the coffee/tea breaks, and:

a. Never talk meaningfully, or for lengthy periods, to any delegate whom you suspect of having an understanding of the session topic.

b. Should such conversations prove unavoidable, pretend to search through your documents for a relevant paper and 'accidentally' spill coffee on their shoes. (Note: This ploy only works effectively once per conference.)

4. Carefully rehearse at least three differing opinions on the Conference topic. Use them sparingly and only as a last resort when in the company of a large group of delegates. If invited to elaborate on your views, take a large bite of the peanut butter covered canapé that you have previously secreted about your person.

5. Make a point of being seen at least once a day in the lobbies of the major, 5-star, delegate hotels. Raise your profile by periodically arranging to have yourself paged. (This is best accomplished by telephoning which ever hotel you happen to be in from one of their public 'phones. Explain to the operator that you understand (*insert own name*), is with a group of people in the bar/restaurant/coffee lounge and that it is imperative that they call head office immediately for an up-dated schedule of their Ministerial appointments.)

6. When taking refreshments ensure that you sit in a well-lit

spot in full view of passing delegates. Maintain a concerned expression and constantly check your watch. This will indicate that the person(s) with whom you had obviously arranged a meeting is/are running late and may cause you to miss the next session.

7.Retain every piece of literature relating to the conference. Hopefully this will be sufficient to fill your suitcase, leaving little room for presents. (The buying of gifts while attending a diving event is discouraged. To do so indicates that you had some leisure time and said gift may be interpreted as a salve to your conscience for some minor indiscretion!)

8.Inevitably you will meet delegates who are "tired and emotional", usually in the cocktail bar of hotels in the late evening. Seek out those delegates whom you deem to be the most "emotional" and remind them of their offer to buy you dinner. On your return the company accountant will commend you for your thrift, thus paving the way for your attendance at the next conference.

9.In the event that your spouse/co-habitant insists on accompanying you:

a.Downgrade your hotel reservation. Take all meals in your hotel room.

b.Attend every session and refuse to acknowledge any member of the opposite sex who may greet you.

c.Spend each evening reviewing the speaker notes and insist

that the mini-bar be removed from your room as not being conducive or relevant to a diving related event.

10. On your return write a tediously lengthy report emphasising the 'Boring' session, (see 2. b above) and, when asked to comment on the Dive Show, plant your tongue firmly in your cheek and tell the truth. "It was bloody hard work!"

CHAPTER 34
DEEP THOUGHTS

If Archimedes had taken a shower instead of a bath then it might have been centuries before somebody else came along and defined the principles of buoyancy!

It was the sort of random thought that sometimes pops into my head when I'm standing under the shower. On this occasion the thought processes received a boost when, looking up to see if the ceiling needed repainting, twin jets of water shot right up both nostrils and prompted a coughing and spluttering fit similar to what I imagine a near-drowning experience must feel like.

Of course, a bloke of Archimedes calibre would probably have made something more of this modest discovery and run out of the bathroom shouting something like, "*Eu* .. (cough-splutter) ... *reka! I have* ... (more hacking throat noises) ...*it*!" and convinced everybody else in the household that he'd either found an underarm deodorant that really worked, or that he'd contracted some horrible disease!

Nevertheless, it did start me thinking about the advantages

of baths and how deep one would need to be before the water lapped up to the level of my nose? A train of thought that in turn led me to the conclusion that what seems to be lacking in diving is a clear definition of many of the terms in common usage.

Take the word, *'deep'*, for example. We all have a subjective view of what is meant by 'deep', but ask any group of divers for a precise definition of the word and the chances are that the answers will vary enormously. It is, after all, a relative term.

During the nineteenth century, anyone who worked underwater wearing a helmet, suit, lead boots and heavy weights was, to the layperson, a deep-sea diver – even if they were only in 3-metres of water! With the introduction of decompression tables it began to be assumed that deep diving only applied to depths greater than 10-metres, the point at which decompression obligations became an issue. The 10-metre demarcation line received a further boost following oxygen toxicity experiments on Navy divers using O_2 rebreathers.

Assuming that the body could safely tolerate a partial pressure of oxygen up to 2 atmospheres absolute, those Royal Navy divers trained on oxygen rebreathers to a maximum depth of 10-metres were designated as 'Shallow Water Divers'.

Air, of course, has it's own problems. Principally nitrogen narcosis, an often debilitating condition that – depending on individual tolerance – can become noticeable at depths beyond 18-metres. In 1953, recognising the problems imposed by narcosis as well as the then existing limitations of carrying an adequate supply of gas, Cousteau suggested a depth restriction of 40-metres for divers using SCUBA; an arbitrary figure supported by the U.S. Navy's recommendations on SCUBA diving operations.

These depth parameters have since been adopted by many of the recreational diver training organizations, with 18-metres now the starting point for 'deep diver' training and 40-metres the generally recommended maximum depth limit for recreational diving.

Neither of which depths adequately defines, 'deep' diving. Try telling a Technical Diver that you're a qualified 'Deep Diver' when the deepest you've ever been is 21-metres, and the chances are that your reputation as somebody who's worth listening to will be sullied forever!

Not that knowledge or understanding of physics and physiology is a pre-requisite to performing dives beyond the 40-metre recreational diving limit. Thanks to technology and techniques pioneered by those who had a set purpose in diving to extreme depths, recreational dives to 70-metres and beyond have become almost commonplace; particularly with the widespread adoption of trimix.

Even those individuals and technical training agencies that previously advocated the use of air as the breathing medium in deeper dives have begun to recognise the advantages in adding a squirt or two of helium to the mix. Especially when it assists in the establishment of a depth record.

Not everybody agrees with me, of course, but I've long held the view that trying to set a depth record on SCUBA for no other purpose than to have your name listed in the Guinness Book of Records, is not dissimilar to stuffing one or two half-starved ferrets down your trousers: the risks are great, and there's a very real danger that critically important body parts may not survive the experience intact!

It's not even a case of, "boldly going where no man has gone before." (I'm referring to the depth thing, not to letting live ferrets loose in your underwear!) Commercial divers regularly spend hours working at greater depths than those ever achieved by SCUBA divers.

The upshot of all of this is that enormous numbers of recreational divers and dive leaders have become very blasé about regularly diving to depths that were once regarded as deep. Which is not to suggest that there's no point in performing deep dives. After all, part of the adventure of diving is in executing properly planned, mission-oriented dives of discovery. Rather, it's to highlight the fact that until such time as we sprout gills there's no such thing as a simple dive and that all dives, regardless of depth, deserve to be treated seriously.

And just to bring this back to buoyancy - when I'm neutrally buoyant and floating at eye level, the tip of my nose is 5 centimetres below the surface of the waves; and when I'm standing upright on the seabed, my nostrils are 170-centimetres above the soles of my feet. I figure that's as good a reason as any for taking the cautious approach and regarding any depth of water greater than 1.7-metres as 'deep diving'!

CHAPTER 35
BITING THE HAND THAT FEEDS YOU

Just so that there's no doubt in anybody's mind about where I stand on the issue, let me put it on record that I'm all in favour of the environment; I like it, and – as far as I'm concerned – the world's a much better place with an environment than without one!

Having now made my position absolutely clear, I'd better point out that, in the past, I never gave the environment much thought. A firm believer in the notion perpetrated by generations of Chief Petty Officers (who took exception to ship's decks being littered with rubbish) that the ocean was the 'world's biggest ashtray', I always assumed that the sea was more than capable of dealing with anything that I happened to throw its way. Even the term 'environment' only meant the difference between being on the spray-soaked bow of a boat, or sitting in a dockside bar whose atmosphere was thick with cigarette smoke and the fumes of spilt beer.

Over the years – and successfully resisting all attempts by environmentalists to win me over to their cause – I remained a happy victim of ignorance and apathy.

To be fair, my attitude was coloured by the belief that environmentalists were some sort of fanatical sect who urged new recruits to run around naked in forests with the occasional pause to give rough-barked trees a big hug.

Not only was I not prepared to rip off my Mickey Mouse boxer shorts in front of strangers, but I also had to consider the potential for serious injury. (The thought of another naked tree-hugger offering to remove splinters from crucial parts of my anatomy with a small pair of tweezers seemed to me a poor way of winning hearts and minds.)

Once I discovered that it was OK to keep your clothes on and still be an environmentalist, I became much more receptive to their aims, particularly with regard to the oceans. Easing myself gently into the conservation cause – and committing to a small, tax-deductible monthly payment – I joined a campaign to Save the Whales under the impression that it was some sort of marine mammal 'adoption' programme. I waited for the organisation to assign me a whale of my very own.

Months went by without so much as a, *'thank you for the pilchards'* postcard from the ungrateful critters, and nothing to show for my concern other than a wardrobe full of 'Save the Whale' 'T'-shirts. (All of which, I later decided, had probably been made in third-world countries for subsistence level wages on hand driven sewing machines lubricated with whale oil!)

Although I still like to think that my passive financial support played a small role in helping prevent the extinction of a species, it did slowly occur to me that few of us ever consider the big picture when it comes to the environment – or the impact of our seemingly good intentions.

During dives, I used to think nothing of hacking open sea urchins and feeding the contents to swarms of appreciative fish. I only stopped when it was pointed out to me that I was interfering with the natural order of things and that sea urchins played an important role in the life cycle of reefs by, among other things, grazing on algae that would otherwise quickly spread and stifle the reef.

It was a seemingly reasonable argument that I accepted until another conservation group – alarmed by the proliferation of crown-of-thorns starfish munching their way through the coral of Australia's Great Barrier Reef – advocated an eradication programme in which divers are employed to inject the creatures with poison!

Having previously been opposed to the practice of cyanide fishing and now beginning to wonder whether the environmental movement was operating on a full set of solar powered batteries, I turned my attention to more aesthetic issues, quickly discovering that there's even a downside to the increasingly well-supported, Ocean Clean-Up days.

Dumping vehicles, unwanted household appliances, bottles, cans and old car tyres into the ocean is something that most of us condemn - unless you happen to be an environmentalist who believes in the ecological benefits of sinking surplus warships in order to create artificial reefs.

On the other hand, removing rubbish that's been allowed to accumulate on the seabed over the course of decades can - unless it's tackled selectively and with great care - have a devastating effect on the marine life by denying them refuge and shelter; a consequence that's sometimes overlooked by those eco-friendly souls who want me to join them in plucking every piece of man-made refuse out of the ocean.

I may have missed a vital chapter somewhere in the eco-instruction manual, but it does seem to me that in constantly urging divers to become active in protecting the ocean environment, we're actually adding to its woes. Which is why, I've decided to become more conscientious and caring by doing nothing!

I'm not going to eat sharks; I'm not going to collect shells; I'm not going to encourage the trade in 'souvenirs-of-the-sea' by buying products made, for example, from turtle-shell, or by consuming any other endangered species; I'm not going to use 'traditional' medicines whose efficacy in restoring lost libidos relies on harvesting vast quantities of otherwise inedible seahorses; I'm not going to feed fish - unless it's an involuntary response brought on by the motion of a heaving vessel in rough seas! I'm not going to throw anything into the ocean and - with the exception of plastic bags and other obvious pollutants - I probably won't remove anything, either.

Based on the fact that the residual effects of vitamins, medications, pills, potions, beer and liverwurst can apparently spell doom and cause as much harm as poor buoyancy control to the breeding cycles of fragile eco-systems, I'm even going to forgo the self-indulgent practice of peeing in my wetsuit while I'm swimming around coral reefs!

Doing something for the environment by doing nothing might seem like a reactionary approach to the cause of conservation, but after years of imposing my values on an environment that needs me less than I need it, I'm prepared to pay more than lip service to the diving mantra, "Take only memories and leave only bubbles".

CHAPTER 36
THE COLD WAR

It's easy to tell the seasoned travellers aboard an aircraft; they're the ones who, when the captain announces, "Cabin staff close all doors and cross check", immediately begin reading a book or magazine, studiously ignore the safety briefing, and only emerge from their cocoon of apparent indifference when the drinks trolley approaches. In that regard alone, flying and diving have a lot in common.

Having once been stung by a swooping bumble bee - and then been told that, according to the Laws of Physics, the creature's general shape and weight renders it incapable of flight - I've always been slightly wary about being cooped up in a large aircraft flying ten thousand metres or so above the ground. Especially when the major items of safety equipment – a lifejacket and an oxygen mask – seem to be more in keeping with escape from a submarine.

Which is one of the reasons why I pay attention to the crewmember's briefing. Apart from anxiously hoping that they'll point out where they hide the parachutes, I'm also curious to see whether any of the airlines ever take up my suggestion of including sensors above each seat that, following a succession of sniffs, snorts and sneezes from passengers with colds, will trigger the release of a large box of tissues from the same overhead space where they stow the oxygen masks.

It seems that whenever I'm going on a dive trip involving air travel, I usually wind up being seated next to a stranger with no handkerchief and whose sinuses are hopelessly out of control.

When diving, of course, what people do with their excess mucous is, quite literally, between them and their facemask, (and in any event is nothing that the judicious use of a handful of seawater before climbing back on board the boat can't cure.) But in the close confines of an aircraft cabin – where there's no escape from all the bugs and viruses that haven't been vacuumed up by the constant gurgling power-snorts of the passenger seated next to me – I live in fear that one or other of the little bug-gers will find my nasal passages more attractive than those of their previous owner, set up shop, and then develop into a full blown cold that'll prevent me from diving.

It's a constant concern of mine, and one that leads me to think that far too much emphasis is placed on the problems associated with flying **after** diving, and not enough thought given to what can happen while you're up there in the air **before** going diving; not least, the risk of catching that most common of all contra-indications to diving fitness, a cold!

For a diver, a cold can be either a curse or a Godsend. Although I've never had to put it to the test, (and I doubt its wisdom anyway) it often used to be said that it was possible to dive with a broken arm or leg but catch a cold and it would stuff up your whole diving day.

On the other hand, faced with the prospect of either getting up early to battle through rough seas before plunging into cold, dark water, or spending longer in bed, I've always found it remarkably easy to claim that, "as buch as I want to do this dibe, I cart 'cause by dose is blocked!"

Coping with a cold is something that most divers will have to deal with at some time during their diving career. How they choose to handle it will differ enormously – especially when the onset of symptoms coincide with the start of a long-planned dive vacation. Unwilling to forgo a few days diving, and prepared to run the risks associated with possible congestion in the lungs and Eustachian tubes, some divers turn to pills, potions and folk remedies to allay the discomfort.

"You should try my remedy for colds," an unsympathetic friend recently advised. "Just go diving and snarf some saltwater up your nose. It works every time!"

As he was an underwater welder rather than a medical practitioner, it wasn't advice that I was prepared to put to the test. (Especially in light of an earlier bad experience when, during the course of a dive, I'd inadvertently managed to inhale a quantity of seawater. Later that day, while trying to impress a good-looking girl by convincing her that my only interest in her body was as a stepping-stone to her mind, my natural charm and wit took a tumble when all of the salt water that I'd previously inhaled decided that it had had enough of my sinuses and exited the system straight into the cup of coffee that I was raising to my lips!)

More widespread, however, is the use by divers of decongestants as an aid in equalisation. Usually in the form of nasal sprays or tablets many of these preparations contain antihistamines or pseudoephedrine, whose side effects, among other things, may cause anxiety, vertigo, drowsiness, a heightened susceptibility to nitrogen narcosis, and even increase the risk of oxygen toxicity, (especially when breathing oxygen enriched mixtures.)

Seldom considered a life-threatening illness on the surface, the common cold – and the remedies used to treat it - can be just that when the desire to dive over-rules common sense.

Which is why, when I have a cold, I prefer to stick to my old Dad's remedy of putting myself to bed, staying warm, and drinking lots of hot milk, honey and whiskey, (the hot milk and honey being optional!) It's a far more comfortable place to be than sitting in an aircraft – and I can sniff and snort to my heart's content without offending anybody else's aesthetic sensibilities!

CHAPTER 37
SURVIVAL OF THE FITTEST

Had diving been an option when Chuck Darwin set out in the *'Beagle'* on that scientific voyage of discovery that paved the way for his theory of evolution, then there's a strong possibility that he may have scrapped the whole notion of natural selection and the survival of the fittest.

In Darwin's day, just going to sea was a risky business and the main reason that many early sailors never bothered about learning how to swim – mainly on the grounds that if their vessel foundered then it was better to drown quickly than to drift around in the vain hope of rescue. (A piece of trivia that gives new meaning to that old saying about the days of, "wooden ships and *iron* men".)

Even taking to the ship's boats or cobbling together a raft from bits of flotsam was, they maintained, just a stopgap measure. Unless the survivors were close to land, then there was little likelihood of chance rescue by a passing ship - and almost certain death from exposure, dehydration and starvation.

Not that all shipwrecked mariners were quite so fatalistic about their chances of survival. Then, as now, tales of the sea were filled with incredible accounts of people who were rescued after spending months adrift at sea in a boat or raft; and who managed to survive on nothing more than rainwater collected in a sail, supplemented by a diet of raw fish and the odd morsel sliced from the fatted calf of a hapless cabin-boy.

In modern times, being lost at sea isn't necessarily the same ordeal that it once was. (Not least for the fact that ration-packs are far more appetising and easier to digest than a well-fed cabin boy!)

Take, for example, the situation of a Frenchman attempting to row single-handedly across the Atlantic, from Newfoundland to Europe. He was a week out from land when his small craft capsized. Unable to right the upturned boat, he used a satellite phone to call his mother in France. She called the French coastguard, who contacted the American coastguard, who subsequently rescued the distressed rower.

Now, thanks to communications satellites, Global Positioning Systems and sophisticated, long-range, search-and-rescue craft, the chances of finding a person missing at sea have improved considerably.

That's not to suggest that the experience is any the less terrifying for those concerned. It still is. It's just a long-winded way of getting round to the fact that many people planning adventure activities place far too much faith in technology and overlook the simple, common-sense approaches towards safely surviving what should be an otherwise enjoyable experience.

Consider recreational diving. Because everyone's had it drummed into them that diving is an, 'equipment intensive activity', there's a tendency to concentrate on the hardware and to relegate to second place the really important things like planning, health, fitness, training and technique.

My mate, Krabbmann – who has strong views about everything – disagreed.

"Science and engineering is what diving's all about." He said, perched on his usual stool in the front bar of, 'The Sozzled Cod', and already two-and-a-half sheets into the wind after several glasses from his private stock of *'Old Cobblers'*. "You can argue all you like about fitness, attitude and skill proficiency, but they're no substitute for soundly engineered equipment items specifically designed for the most extreme diving conditions.

"The fact is", he continued, "that technology's opened up a whole new world and made it possible for almost anyone who's able to breathe in and out for themselves to go diving in perfect safety. And you can forget all of those doubts and concerns about decompression illness. Thanks to sophisticated dive computers capable of calculating every aspect of the dive and that tell the diver what to do and when to do it, that's no longer an issue. Just follow the advice of your computer and it's impossible to come to harm!"

"What?" I spluttered. "But ... but ..."

Ignoring my attempted interruption, Krabbmann carried on down the slippery slope. "You've got to start facing up to the facts; survival in diving now depends on technology."

"... but things can still go wrong and equipment can always fail." I managed to squeeze in.

"That's what buddies are for!" Said Krabbmann – who's been experiencing great difficulty of late in finding somebody who's prepared to dive with him. "If you do run into any sort of difficulty, their job is to bail you out of the mess and ensure your safety. Not that it should ever be necessary with the new developments in equipment design."

Darwin might have been inclined to disagree. In his day, technology was a tool. Not the substitute for water-confidence, training and mental aptitude that, for some divers, it subsequently seems to have become!

CHAPTER 38
HEAR TODAY, GONE TOMORROW

With so much emphasis placed on sleek equipment design and technology, divers tend to give greater priority to things like face masks and fins than they do to their more important biological bits and pieces. Take ears, for example. Most of us can go for days at a time without even thinking about them. Which is remarkably sad when you consider how much attention we pay to the latest fin or regulator design.

It's not the sort of thing that divers will readily admit to, but most of them do take pride in having equipment that sparks envy in others. And because their safety and well-being depends on that piece of gear functioning perfectly at all times, they protect their investment with a proper care and maintenance programme.

Part of the reason for this is, of course, the fact that equipment items come with their own price tag attached, whereas ears tend to be free as part of an all-inclusive package deal. With no apparent economic worth, they go largely unnoticed when contrasted with a new and expensive piece of diving equipment.

"'Cor! Is that one of those new Quantum regulators you've got there? That's the one with the slide-mounted woofter valve and double-barrelled, spring-loaded giggling pin, isn't it? It's supposed to really improve gas delivery performance. By the way, I like your ears!"

For some reason, ears seldom receive the same sort of acknowledgement as do other parts of the body. People notice facial features and things like hairstyle and colour - and the shape of Kylie Minogue's bum - but seldom pay any attention at all to the ears. (Unless they're large and happen to stick out at right-angles to the head; in which case the owners usually get stuck with brutal nick-names like 'Wing-nut', or 'Dumbo'!)

At a personal level, I've always appreciated the value of ears! They've proven to be remarkably useful things for preventing hats falling down over the eyes, holding sunglasses in place, or knowing when somebody has offered to buy me a beer – a primary function of ears and one that has lots of other useful applications.

But despite their prominent place in all diving 101 texts, ears rarely get the sort of respect due to such delicate and sensitive instruments. Which is hardly surprising given that all of the tiny fiddly bits have robust names like anvil, stirrup, hammer and drum; designations that make them sound as though they more properly belong on the shop floor of a busy iron foundry.

(Which is probably the reason why so many people carry out regular excavation surveys of their ear cavities using things like pens, pencils and even straightened out paper-clips, and ignore the sage advice to never poke anything into their ear that's smaller than their elbow!)

Caring for their ears is something that most divers acknowledge, but few actually practice to the point where they're prepared to have them checked periodically by a diving physician. Even using cotton buds, or a finger, to remove wax is fraught with problems. Forming a waterproof covering that protects the skin of the outer ear canal, there's a danger that the wax will be pushed inwards to form a plug that prevents proper equalisation. And if the protective wax coating is removed, there's a risk that organisms that thrive in warm, moist environments will set up home and create their own painful problems.

Although it's a seemingly simple act to perform, equalisation isn't always easy. Particularly when the diver is suffering from even minor 'stuffiness' as the result of, say, a mild head cold and when, because of limited vacation time, they are determined to dive at all costs. Often using more force than is wise – or necessary – in order to achieve equalisation, the diver can cause damage to the ear drum with long term consequences in terms of hearing loss. And that's leaving to one side all of the other affects that a mix of differential air and water pressure, temperature, wax and mucous can have on the ear's well-being – or the role that the mechanism also plays in balance and orientation.

All divers quickly learn that the easiest way to save face when they have doubts about a particular dive is to claim an inability to, 'clear their ears'! While it's a handy excuse, it is – regrettably – the only time that many of them pay any heed to the health of those overlooked appendages!

Not that it worries my mate, 'Wing-nut'. He's of the opinion that ears make great stabilisers. Krabbmann, on the other hand, is one of those evolutionary-theorist divers who believe that ears are the vestigial remains of gills: He take's great delight in telling people with opinions that differ from his own to, "Blow it out your ears!"

I'm the only sensible one among the three of us. I have this fear that if I subject my ears to too much abuse then I'll never hear that offer to buy me a beer!

CHAPTER 39
AT THE GOING DOWN OF THE SUN ...

"Do not go gentle into that goodnight
Old age should burn and rave at close of day;
Rage, rage against the dying of the light."

- Dylan Thomas

For reasons that are obvious to everyone who knows me, I always try to avoid looking into mirrors. And even on those occasions when it does become necessary, (like having to stick bits of toilet tissue on razor cuts) I seldom focus on the B-I-G picture. As a consequence, I've managed to retain a mental image of myself as I once was some umpteen decades ago: A time before wrinkles were first invented and when I had the physique – and temperament – of a half-starved barracuda!

There is, I suppose, a little bit of the *'Dorian Grey'* in all of us; an unwillingness to recognise the slow and subtle changes wrought by time and a need to keep the past alive by putting a slightly different twist on the facts. It was something that I hadn't thought too deeply about until I attended a recent social gathering of the Hysterical Divers Society, held in the front bar of '*The Sozzled Cod*'.

It was one of those functions where everybody stands around with a drink in one hand and a cocktail-sausage-on-a-toothpick in the other while dredging up impossible stories about diving's "good old days" and how – unlike today's new breed of divers - a person had to be tough, intelligent and committed to make the grade.

My mate Krabbmann was in his element. "In those days," he said, "buddy-breathing from a twin-hose regulator demanded real skill; getting 'narced' was all part of the thrill, and we all had to be fearless to survive. Not like the cosseted and mollycoddled divers that are churned out today."

Because we were all looking backwards down a time-tunnel at the people we would have liked to be, (and probably never were) none of us openly disagreed with him. But tucked away in the back of my mind was this niggling thought that I couldn't actually recall being 'fearless'!

I still cringe, for example, when I think of my first night dive. It was 1963 and only a short way into the Royal Navy's lengthy diving programme. The dive took place from a boat hovering over a seemingly bottomless hole in the floor of the English Channel. It was winter, the seas were rough and the sleet was blowing sideways when the Petty Officer asked for the first volunteer. "You'll do, Strike!" I was kitted up with surface demand diving equipment, a pair of lead boots and instructed to descend 120-feet down a suspended shot-line and practice line signals with the surface tender.

With no light, I slowly made my way down the line to spend

what seemed like hours – but was in reality only minutes – answering pulls on the lifeline. It was pitch black and I couldn't see a thing, (mainly 'cause my eyes were tight shut with fear) while I waited for the signal to ascend and, as I'd now determined, quit the course.

Back on the boat, my shivering and teeth-chattering symptoms of terror were put down to the cold. Before I could recover enough to tell anyone of my decision to pull out of the course, the Petty Officer decided that conditions were too rough to continue night diving and we returned to the base.

I eventually passed the course, earning (to my way of thinking) every penny of the increased pay that I subsequently received. It was only later, with the confidence borne of increased experience that I began to enjoy every moment spent underwater.

Listening to the folk gathered in the bar of '*The Sozzled Cod*' that evening, it suddenly dawned on me that we'd become the same silly old fossils that we used to scoff at when we were younger. And that our collective experiences – although very modest when weighed against the achievements of today's supposedly 'cosseted and molly-coddled' divers - were not so very different from those that divers will always encounter.

The truth is, the 'good old days' really weren't that good. It's just that some people prefer the certainty of the past and secretly envy those younger generations who will be exposed to all of diving's future possibilities.

"We even had to make our own wet suits using paper patterns and sheets of un-lined neoprene held together with glue, tape and faith." Krabbmann continued.

Considering the expansive effects of age, it occurred to me that most of the people in the room would require at least five-times as much neoprene if they still had to make their own wet-suits.

Not me, of course!

CHAPTER 40
SHAPE UP OR SHIP OUT

In successfully distancing recreational diving from the military-style teaching methods of yesteryear, the training organizations seem to have overlooked the economic potential of 'boot-camp' style fitness programmes that emphasise the *'no pain, no gain'* philosophy!

For the benefit of those who are unfamiliar with the concept, it's a relatively recent phenomenon; one in which people who are apparently incapable of motivating themselves, crawl out of bed at sparrow-fart and pay somebody with all of the delicate sensibilities of a psychopathic drill sergeant heaps of money to scream at them and threaten to rip their bloody arms off and beat them to death with the soggy stumps if they don't immediately perform fifty push-ups!

Having spent some years on the receiving end of this sort of treatment (albeit in a paid capacity and managing to survive the experience with all of my appendages intact), I rather like the idea of switching roles and being the one who gets to dish out insults and do all of the shouting. It is, in fact, the sort of job that I'd be prepared to give somebody else's right arm for – and the left one too if it meant more money!

And judging by the growing demand for fitness programmes of this type, there's a small fortune to be made for the first organisation prepared to go out on a limb by turning back the clock and structuring an entry-level course based on some of the earlier methods of diver selection and training.

It won't, of course, be an easy course to pass, but in restricting it to people with healthy bank balances and low self-esteem, it'll give a healthy boost to dive store profit margins. And, by limiting the numbers of people actually certified as divers, give even greater credibility to diving's already impressive record for safety.

Immediately precluded from the entry-level diver training course will be – as in diving's early days - those people with, '*short necks, full blooded and florid complexions.*' people who are: '*very pale, whose lips are more blue than red, who are subject to cold hands and feet and who have what is commonly called a languid circulation.*' Or those who are, '*hard drinkers and have suffered repeatedly and severely from venereal disease or who have rheumatism or sunstroke.*'

"Listen up, sea-slug! These selection standards are for your benefit. Don't try telling me that two out of four ain't bad! Unless, that is, you want to spend the rest of the day standing in that garbage-bin shouting, 'I am rubbish.' Divers on my course are – or should be - people of, '*good physique and capable of enduring considerable bodily and mental strain. If possible, persons who have a strong team spirit and an alert sense of responsibility ...*

the lone wolf is never a success in the diving world, either above or below the water.'

"And 'cause I'm a nice bloke, I'm not even going to mention the bit about divers being required to be, *'above average intelligence'*!

"What we're looking for are people with, *'no history of nervous breakdowns, irresponsible behaviour, or fits. Addiction to alcohol is also undesirable as it indicates mental instability and inability to stand sustained mental or physical strain. Heavy smokers are (also) not usually suitable'.*"

"But I saw you down at the, *'Floppy Flounder'* pub the other night, dancing on the tables with a full beer glass in each hand, your shorts around your ankles and bent over with a smouldering cigarette stuck ... Can you bounce that bit about, *'physical strain'* past me just one more time?"

"Don't give me any of that lip, you little piece of shark-snot. All certified divers that have been through the hoops like what I have, know that it's OK to let your shorts - I mean, your hair - down now and again. But that's a privilege reserved for us what have been there and done that. And one that you – as a new conscript to diving – are going to have to earn the hard way!

"And don't think for one moment that I've forgotten how old you are! You're a borderline case as far as age is concerned. You knew when you paid your money and signed on for this course that, *'as a general rule, people over 30-years of age should not be selected for training as divers. Trained divers can continue for some years after this age, but must be watched carefully as they enter their late thirties. Divers beyond the age of 45 ought not to be employed on deep diving or in any work involving long stays under pressure. People who are overweight should be rejected. It is said that they are more prone to the bends, but what is more important is that they are not fit for arduous diving.'*

"Now plop your over-weight carcass back into that pool, you slimy pile of squid droppings, and give me ten more mask clearings before I even consider teaching you the intricacies of regulator recovery techniques. You hear me?"

Based on its success in other areas of physical pursuits, it's a programme with obvious benefits as far as the image of diving is concerned. All that's needed is the widespread support of all of those Training Agency people who've failed to keep abreast of popular trends, and who still believe that diving should be an enjoyable activity. But that's something that - after a week or two of diver 'boot-camp' training - can easily be beaten out of them!

CHAPTER 41
THE GEE! SPOT

Back in the days when I used to think a lot about virginity, I always regarded it as a – hopefully – temporary condition somewhat similar to having the chicken pox or measles, an ailment that, if the sufferer was lucky, could be quickly cured. (The alternative – according to some cultures – was to be pushed to the front of the queue, as a sacrificial offering should a volcanic vent ever pop up in the backyard and threaten to spew boiling-hot lava all over mum's prize-winning petunia patch.)

Nowadays, (having survived chicken pox, measles and the inconveniently-placed back-seat springs of an old Austin 8 car) whenever I hear the word *'virgin'*, I always begin to think about diving. And before anyone suggests that I need several-hundred volts worth of electric shock therapy, it's not quite as bizarre as it sounds. I know people who, whenever the word *'diving'* is mentioned start thinking about warm, woolly socks, après-dive mugs of hot chocolate, or the molecular properties of various exotic gases.

In my case, however, it's simple word association based on the various meanings of the term 'virgin' and the fact that it usually implies being untouched, faultless, flawless, pure, immaculate and ... and ... ***pristine***!

And it's the word 'pristine' that gets right up my starboard nostril.

Read a sufficient number of articles or brochures promoting exotic diving destinations and there's a better than even chance that the word 'pristine' is going to crop up somewhere or other in a variation of, *"We sank down through the azure blue, our bubbles rising above us like a silver screen as we descended onto the pristine reef below ..."* (and it's almost certain that once you stumble across the word *'pristine',* you'll find *'kaleidoscopic'* and *'myriad'* somewhere close by) *"... where a myriad of kaleidoscopically coloured marine life greeted our arrival'.* (I told you so.)

It's not that there's anything wrong with the word 'pristine'. In the right context it's a perfectly adequate word to describe something that, in the words of the Oxford English Dictionary, is, *"Ancient, primitive, unspoilt."* But in the case of diving it's become an over-used word that's acquired a whole raft of new and different meanings. Especially when it comes to deciding on a destination based solely on advertising literature and reports describing the dive sites.

Tell somebody that a place offers a variety of outstanding reef and wall diving rich in marine life and it's reasonable to assume that that is what's on offer, without the need for other vague superlatives. But tell them that a diving destination is *'pristine'*, (one that's presumably unspoilt and where divers have had absolutely no impact whatsoever on the diving environment) and it's like baiting a crab-pot with a lump of old flounder.

THE GEE! SPOT

Which is exactly what drew my mate, Krabbmann to a remote island speck out in the middle of the ocean to join a small group of experienced divers privileged to be among the first to dive and photograph a newly discovered wreck of supposedly historical significance.

"To my of thinking", he said, on his return, "an aluminium-hulled dinghy that sank in the last cyclone and that's half-buried in silt at a depth of 10-metres, doesn't measure up to what I expect from a wreck-dive described as, '*a recently discovered vessel in pristine condition*'.

"Mind you, it's easy to see why the whole place is unspoilt. Unless you're one of those people who find inspiration in flat, featureless expanses of silt and sand, there's absolutely nothing worth seeing there!

"And as for any, 'historical significance' - the fact that the dinghy once belonged to a person who knew a person who claimed to be a descendant of Nelson doesn't really put it up there alongside the *'President Coolidge'* as a dive tourism attraction!"

Although I still like the idea of discovering - and diving – reefs, wrecks and dive sites that nobody else has ever visited or seen, today I am more mindful of the fact that any place that's described as 'pristine' may well lack the qualities that make some diving destinations worth re-visiting time and time again.

"Anyway" Said Krabbmann. "I've certainly learned a lesson. Never again will I be lured into visiting a place purely on the basis that the diving attractions are supposedly 'pristine'.

"My next dive trip is to this place I've just read about that's described as having, '*a melange of marine life.*' I don't know what a bloody 'melange' is, but it sounds far more exciting than that place where you enjoy diving all of the time."

"Gee!" I said. "I hope there's just as broad a variety of marine life as we see each week on our own doorstep."

CHAPTER 42
THE EVIL AYE

Despite the objections of sceptics, lots of folks like to keep their options open when it comes to superstitions. It's probably a hangover from childhood when we still believed that there might be magic in the world. Nevertheless, there are lots of otherwise seemingly rational people who still avoid breaking mirrors, walking under ladders, or stepping on cracks in the pavement for fear that to do so will attract bad luck. On the other hand there are certain talismans that are said to bring good luck.

With our recent planned dives cancelled by bad weather, Sylvia handed me a list of chores that I'd previously managed to avoid. *"That's just my bad luck."* I thought, as I begrudgingly began weeding the garden. Plucking out a bunch of clover, I suddenly realised that one of them had four leaves! *"Wow!"* I thought. *"That's surely a sign of Good Luck!"* I slipped the leaf into my wallet and left it to work its magic.

The following morning my computer blew up, taking with it all of my records that I'd failed to back up. I bought a new computer and new software and then spent two weeks trying to configure the thing. *"It's only a piece of machinery"*, I said to myself, *"and no match for half-a-million years of evolutionary development."* It was! I relented and called in a friend who's an expert in these things. He managed to fix everything in two-hours flat.

I told a Scottish friend my tale of woe. He explained to me that four-leaf clovers are only lucky if you happen to be Irish - which I'm not! I believed him and flushed the cloverleaf down the loo. The following morning the cistern fell off the wall and shattered to bits. I had to buy a new one and then pay a plumber to install it.

Thinking logically about all that had happened, the rational part of my mind assured me that my chance finding of an unusual plant leaf had absolutely no bearing on the subsequent spell of 'bad luck'. Nevertheless, I couldn't help thinking that perhaps fickle fate had just given me the finger!

My friend, Dr. Gretta Wrassebender – a person who was denied admission to the Society of Sceptics when she refused to attend one of their Friday 13th meetings – was unsympathetic.

"That's no more than you deserve for believing in superstitious hocus-pocus rather than well established and scientifically proven fact," she said. "And it's not the sort of thinking that has any place in diving."

I wasn't altogether convinced that she was playing with a full deck of tarot cards! It's not necessary to look into a crystal ball to realise that with the exception of a few basic Laws of Physics, the majority of divers pay little attention to science preferring instead to rely on faith in what they've read or heard, (but don't necessarily understand!) to keep them safe from harm.

In that regard nothing quite compares with the diving computer as an amulet supposedly capable of warding off 'bad luck'. Seduced by the packaging and the features, many divers have absolute faith in the ability of this one instrument to keep them safe from harm. With no understanding of the fact that a diving computer is just a very sophisticated timing device, their brain switches off at the same time as the computer turns on.

To be fair, I can't claim any expertise in the workings of dive computers. But I did recently ask a world-respected authority on the subject of decompression what were the differences between the various algorithms touted by computer manufacturers.

"That's easy." He said. "It's all a question of mathematical mumbo-jumbo and the selective use of a soldering iron. And you can quote me on that." I have!

It was an honest answer, especially given all that is known about the mechanics of decompression sickness. On the other hand, it does rather echo what - centuries ago - a bloke wearing a tall pointy hat and dark cloak with silver moons emblazoned all over it might have said:

"'ello, young Arfur. I've 'ad a good look at that sword wot that Lady in the Lake gave you the uvver day and I've given it a bit of a tweek by adding a few magic spells of my own. Now there ain't a sword in the land quite like this one. 'ang on tight to it and you'll never come to any 'arm. Serious magic like this would normally set you back two copper coins and a pig's ear, but seein' as 'ow it's you, a private box seat at the jousting tournament will do just fine."

"It'll work then, will it, Merlin? And keep me safe from all possible hurt and injury?"

"Aye, lad. That it will. Just 'ave faith in wot wizard instructors like me tell you and you'll never come to any harm. Mind you, it still won't 'urt to wear a bit of armour!"

CHAPTER 43
COLOUR ME BLUE

Suffering for one's art is a cross that all of us underwater photographers learn to bear. I say "us", because while my talents in this field have never been properly recognised, I've more than paid my dues in terms of anguish and misery.

It's not that I lack any creative ability - despite claims to the contrary by several prominent underwater photographers who've been privileged to see my portfolio of work. It's rather more to do with the fact that every underwater camera and housing that I've ever owned or used has had inherent defects that nobody, other than myself, seems to have recognised.

Lacking the necessary funding to be able to afford an underwater camera of my own, I was given a kick-start by the Navy who, in the mid-'Sixties, made me sign a, *'I-will-pay-for-it-if-I-lose-or-damage-it'* chit for two of the original Calypso cameras (pre-cursor to the Nikonos series) before packing me off to Malta to spend a summer photographing dye trails released on the thermocline interface.

Because of their mechanical simplicity, (and never having

even seen, let alone touched, an underwater camera before) I failed to read the instruction manual properly. Particularly that bit that said: *'Caution: Never unload the camera underwater'*.

It was a temporary set back that, rather than quenching my interest in this emerging art form, made me determined to master all of its intricacies. I read books and articles on underwater photography and, swallowing my pride, even asked experienced U/W photographers for advice.

The first underwater camera that I ever actually owned was a Nikonos V, complete with strobe. It was an easy choice to make considering how many of the world's most prominent U/W photographers - using that same model camera - had attracted fame, fortune and praise for the calibre of their work.

Regrettably, however, my own camera never seemed to produce photographs that measured up to the quality of their images. (And that was only when I actually managed to take pictures that had a recognisable subject matter. For some reason most of my photographs looked as though they were taken in a dark cave at midnight using natural ambient light.)

Resisting the urge to give up on photography, my next discovery was that a Nikonos V held precisely $698 worth of seawater. Just to be certain of this fact, I successfully managed to flood the camera a second time; a process that proved beyond all doubt that water is a precious, (and expensive) commodity!

Having now spent a small fortune on film with no discernible improvement in results, I was beginning to give up hope of ever making the grade as an underwater photographer. But then came the digital camera revolution.

The beauty of digital cameras in underwater housings is that you can immediately check the results. I had mine for three weeks before forgetting to properly clean and check the housing seal. It flooded on the surface. Quickly dousing it in distilled water and drying it gently with a hair-dryer, I found that it still worked - apart from the lens cover occasionally failing to open; a minor inconvenience that I managed to fix by vigorously banging the camera housing against a rock before turning on the power.

It was an effective technique that worked well right up until the regular Saturday morning shore dive when I positioned myself to photograph a seahorse, whacked the camera against a rock to open the lens cover, and then watched water flood into the housing.

Inspired by my earlier successful attempts at resuscitation, I dunked the camera, (that was probably already beyond salvation) into a bucket of fresh water and, quite forgetting just how many plastic components there are in digital cameras, blasted it with hot air from an industrial strength hair-dryer at full throttle. It had all the makings of a great salvage plan up until that moment when parts of the camera began to warp and melt.

"I suppose you'll be buying another – and more advanced – camera now that you've put the old one out of its misery?" Krabbman asked.

"You betcha! Only this time I'm getting one with more goblins."

"Goblins?" Krabbmann queried.

"No! That's wrong, isn't it?" I said. "It's not goblins, it's .. er .. pixies. That's it, pixies. It's how us photographers refer to image quality. That last camera only had 3 mega-pixies – that's big pixies almost the size of gremlins – but the new one that

I'm getting has over 7 mega-pixies. That's more than enough pixies to sort out any gremlins lurking in the camera."

"Goblins, gremlins and pixies!" Krabbmann sneered. "What you need is a pad of paper and a box of crayons rather than a camera."

I didn't like to tell him that I'd already tried that, but the paper kept dissolving and an octopus stole my blue crayon. Photography's much easier!

CHAPTER 44
STAMP OUT COCCOLITHOPHORES – AND PENGUINS

It might be the little things in life that matter, but it's always the big things that get our attention.

Take whales, for example. Weighing in at a staggering 60,000-plus kilograms, (that's about 132,000 pounds for the metrically challenged) the mighty Blue Whale is said to be the largest creature that the world has ever produced. And yet our knowledge of their habits (like that of all whales – including the smaller and more prolific Minke whale) is pitifully small and largely restricted to observations made by early whalers who hunted them almost to the point of extinction.

Outraged by Japan's recent announcement that they intend to hunt both the Minke and Humpback whales for 'scientific' purposes, public opinion has come out strongly in favour of the whales with most people expressing condemnation at such unnecessary slaughter.

That should read, most people apart from my mate, Krabbmann.

"Science and popular opinion seldom see eye to eye," he said. "And when it comes to whales, the question that you should be asking yourself is: what are whales doing for the planet and the environment?

"People get incensed about the de-forestation of the Amazon jungles, claiming that they generate a significant proportion of the world's oxygen and that their destruction spells doom for the earth. They forget that more than 50% of the oxygen in our atmosphere (some sources claim 98%) comes from the phytoplankton in our oceans. That same microscopic plant that provides the food source for zooplankton which, in its turn, is eaten by larger creatures such as krill; the tiny shrimp-like creatures that form the staple diet for baleen whales like the Blue, Humpback and Minke whales. And a big whale can munch their way through up to two tons of the stuff a day!

"Were you aware," Krabbmann continued, "that hundreds of millions of years ago, when life on earth first began, the planet's oxygen levels were as high as 35%! Now look at it; the oxygen content is down to just a little over 20%. If you want my opinion," (I didn't, but I got it anyway) "it's all the fault of the whales and their practice of scoffing down tons of plankton.

"With so many of those little *coccolithophores* and other members of the phytoplankton winding up inside the bellies of whales, it won't be long before we're all asphyxiated. The fact is," he said, "that nobody seems interested in championing the cause of the tiny stuff, regardless of its importance."

Even for Krabbmann, (a person without equal when it comes to making two plus two equal five) it was a lousy defence of whaling; a stance that he attempted to justify by pointing out the impact that an oxygen-enriched atmosphere would have on diving.

"For a start, divers wouldn't need to be convinced that smoking was a health hazard and incompatible with good diving practice - anyone attempting to light a cigarette could kiss goodbye to their eyebrows; nobody would have to fork out extra money on a nitrox course – that'd all be covered in diving 101; there'd be a greater acceptance of mixed gases for deep diving; and the role of narcosis in causing diving 'accidents' would be reduced considerably. And then there's ..."

"Before you get carried away", I interrupted, "you'd better read this report from a scientist who claims that some species of phytoplankton, rather than simply doing what plants do best and using the sun's rays to turn carbon-dioxide into oxygen through photosynthesis - and then reflecting the heat back into space - actually absorb the rays and are contributing to the greenhouse effect and the planet's warming."

"If that's the case" Krabbmann said, in a typical about-face, "then we should be doing all that we can to protect whales and encouraging them to eat more, not condoning their slaughter.

"Penguins, of course, are another matter. All of those black feathers soak up the heat. If they're allowed to breed indiscriminately then there's a very real risk that the Antarctic ice cap will start to melt, causing a rise in sea levels that'll flood out the dive shop."

Sadly, Krabbmann, like many others, gives too little thought to the complexity and magic of life – and the importance of conserving it all!

CHAPTER 45
STUFF AND NONSENSE

Not many people realise that the idea of stuffing olives was hit upon by an obscure sect of Spanish nuns who, when there was a seasonal glut of the things, came up with a neat idea for taking out the pit and substituting it with a pimento. Their stuffed olives proved so popular – and financially rewarding for the convent - that it gave rise to a major industry with, it is said, a good nun being able to stuff up to 600 olives a day.

Needless to say their role in this entrepreneurial venture was soon forgotten when a money-grubbing industrialist mechanised the process and - able to produce more stuffed olives in an hour than a nun could in a day - captured the market and put the convent out of business.

It's the sort of trivia that Krabbmann sometimes comes up with as a prelude to talking about ways of making money out of the diving industry.

"It's sad," he said, "to think of those nuns spending years stuffing olives in order to raise money for charitable purposes, only to have somebody with greater resources capitalise on their discovery and reap all of the rewards. But that's market forces for you.

"Diving's no exception." He continued. "Look at Haldane! The same thing happened to him; except that he spent years stuffing goats into recompression chambers - rather than pimentos into olives - in order to formulate a set of decompression tables that would alleviate the bends.

"Having laid the groundwork, his freely available findings were taken up by later generations of researchers, many of whom developed their own proprietary tables that they now sell at a profit to other users. Stuff happens!" Krabbmann said, philosophically.

Having gone down a similar path, I sympathised with the nuns and Haldane.

As the President of Zymurgy Inc., (an international not-for-profit consortium of diving technologists committed to providing divers with equipment so ahead of its time that no recognisable need for it yet exists) I played a prominent role in the design and development of the world's first Nitrox Snorkel, the 'Uranus'.

With the intention of sharing all of our designs with the entire diving community, we never considered slapping a patent on 'Uranus', a snorkel that, in outward appearance, resembled the 1954, U.S. Divers model; the one with a ping-pong ball valve at its upper end.

With all of the usual characteristics of a conventional snorkel, what set 'Uranus' apart was the inclusion of a membrane adsorbent located in a canister midway along the stem of the snorkel: A mechanism that served to filter unwanted gases from the mix while allowing the operator to select the appropriate oxygen mix via a manually operated spindle valve attached to the reservoir well at the snorkel's lower end.

Unlike modern snorkels, the top of ours curved downwards and was fitted with an open sided 'cage' housing the microchip sensor device, a ping-pong ball shaped instrument that automatically switched the mix to 21% oxygen on the surface.

However, and despite positive comment from that small core group of divers interested in pushing technology to its limits, sales of 'Uranus' weren't even sufficient to cover our R&D costs. (Probably because of our insistence that every purchaser paid an additional fee for the mandatory two-day training course in its use.)

Turning our attention to other more lucrative projects, we told the distributor to "sit on Uranus", and then promptly forgot about it. Until just recently, that is, when another diving organization, realising the enormous profit potential in the compulsory training programme, launched their own version of the Nitrox Snorkel.

A shameless copy employing the same technology as our original design, the only difference between their unimaginatively named, 'E-Snorkel' and the 'Uranus' was the replacement of our manually operated spindle valve with an automated electronic gizmo. An innovation that, they claimed, gave the E-Snorkel greater appeal by eliminating the need for users to think for themselves, thereby reducing the time and cost of training and encouraging more sales.

It was impossible to say who'd been stuffed the most: Zymurgy Inc. for failing to patent the Nitrox Snorkel, or the would-be divers trained to believe that technology really is a replacement for knowledge!

CHAPTER 46
MANUAL DEXTERITY

Hanging on my office wall is a framed copy of *The Times* newspaper dated Thursday, November 7th 1805 carrying the first reports of the Battle of Trafalgar, fought off the Spanish coast on the 21st October of that same year; a dramatic sea battle in which famed naval hero Admiral Lord Nelson died at the moment of victory over the combined French and Spanish fleets.

The despatches, written on the 22nd October and carried by fast schooner back to England, filled the entire newspaper with a detailed account of the battle, news of which had taken over two weeks to filter through to the reading public. It was an age when demand for news of world events outstripped the publisher's ability to print sufficient copies of the four-page newspaper. Queues formed in clubs and coffee-houses to read of the events that had taken place in far-away Spain.

. . .

The point of this historical diversion is to highlight the fact that today it's no longer necessary to forage through rubbish bins searching for a discarded copy of *The Times* in order to keep abreast of world news. Thanks to sophisticated communications technology capable of beaming real-time images and commentary directly into our homes twenty-four hours a day, it's almost impossible to remain ignorant of what's taking place around the globe.

Bombarded with neatly encapsulated summaries of what it is that the media think that we need to know, few people have either the time or the inclination to wade through reams of text for the detail. It's got to the point where even the telephone is becoming obsolete as far as voice communication is concerned.

Captivated by technology, it's now become commonplace for people in the same office to conduct conversations via e-mail rather than lean around the partition and ask for a paper clip. Although it's a growing phenomenon that only adds to the information overload, e-mail does at least have the advantage of encouraging people to express their thoughts and ideas in the written form – and to hopefully read and comprehend what it is that others are saying to them.

Regrettably, however, even e-mail is starting to be overshadowed by the Short Message Service (SMS) capabilities of most mobile 'phones. The non-verbal equivalent of cavemen grunting, snorting and farting to make themselves understood, the SMS syndrome has, in just a short space of time, wiped out several thousand years of literary achievement. It's accomplished this by reducing ideas and concepts to what are essentially coded abbreviations in which people are able to quickly and readily learn *what* is happening – without necessarily understanding *how* or *why*.

Always quick to seize on popular trends that have the potential to make him wealthy, my mate Krabbmann is already catering for the diver of tomorrow by producing a Nu-Speak diving manual divided into sections, each of which can readily be absorbed during a single visit to the bathroom.

With the potential to be a classic of its type, he's allowed me to reproduce various sections of his Dive Manual, beginning with the chapter dealing with some of the Gas Laws:

"Boyls Law

Volum s n invrs prprtion 2 pressr. The depr u go the gra8r the wtr pressr aktng on ur bdy. Gas spces wivn ur bdy wl b cmprsd nles the pressr s ekwlsd.

"Dltn's Law

The prtial pressr of gs in a mxtur wil rmane cnstnt & act ndpndntly of uver gses. As u go depr N_2 bcums nrcotc 2 u. Ths gs tho inrt hs n ansthtic efect.

"Hnrys Law

The solublty of a gs in a likwd or fluid is drectly prprtonl 2 pressr. Suplid by rspration & crclatun N_2 isnt usd by the bdy

& is progrsivly absrbd by ur tissus untl absrbtn ekwvlnt 2 sroundng wtr pressr s achvd."

Some people might consider it to be unnecessarily wordy, but I do believe that the section on dive planning is worth repeating in its entirety – even if only to reinforce its importance to diver safety:

"2dys dve strts the nite b4. Pln ur dve nd dve ur pln. Mke ur nmbr of acnts eql 2 ur dcnts."

A little more succinct is his treatment of decompression.

"Rli n ur cmputr."

There will, of course, be detractors who pooh-pooh Krabbmann's efforts, but given the number of would-be divers who complain about the worth of more orthodox diving manuals – and the difficulty of carrying one when travelling – there's a huge market potential for one that can be stored on a mobile phone!

CHAPTER 47
A LESSON IN LUNACY

I've always enjoyed reading the, 'I-Learned-About-Diving-From-That' type article that pops every now and then in the pages of diving magazines: Dramatic tales about being caught in the "invisible death grip" of a down current; becoming trapped inside the compartment of a wreck; being left at sea; suffering an embolism or 'bend'; coping with an equipment malfunction at depth, or a scary encounter with sharks.

They're the sorts of stories in which readers are encouraged to bare their bums to the world by writing about their diving disasters and near-death experiences, and usually conclude with a short sermon to the effect that in diving nothing should ever be taken for granted.

When they're being honest, most of the writers admit that the incidents were the result of poor dive planning, lack of foresight, or a failure to accept responsibility for their own actions and well being.

Occasionally, however, some divers find it easier to pin the blame for their predicament on somebody else. In extreme cases, (like my mate, Krabbmann when he wants to side-step the issue of responsibility) they'll even suggest that the incident was an Act of God and could have happened to anyone!

"Did I ever tell you about the time, I was Instructing on a day-boat?" Krabbman asked.

"It was my first day on the job," he continued. "I'd given a comprehensive briefing about the dive site and ensured that everybody was familiar with the dive plan. I'd even given a few pointers to one novice diver about ways to make his diving more comfortable based on my own vast experience.

"Within a few minutes of their descent two divers surfaced, one towing his nearly-unconscious and choking buddy back to the boat. Rapidly hauling the afflicted diver out of the water and into the enclosed cockpit where the oxygen cylinder was stored, I quickly discovered what had gone wrong.

"It seems that the novice diver had been overly concerned about the condition that, during the briefing, I'd described as 'cotton-mouth' – the one where your mouth gets all dry on account of the pure dry breathing air delivered by the regulator.

"Deciding to adopt my recommendation of putting a marble in your mouth as an aid to condensation, he had, without my knowledge, helped himself to a handful of my marbles. During his descent – and with a gob full of marbles – he discovered that he couldn't grip the regulator mouthpiece properly. It drifted out of his mouth. While replacing the regulator, he depressed the purge button. An action that forced air – together with one of the marbles – down his throat.

"Quickly assessing the situation," Krabbmann continued, "I performed the Heimlich manoeuvre on the diver in order to dislodge the obstruction. It was so effective that the offending marble – now a lethal projectile - shot out of his mouth, smacked into the GPS and, on the ricochet, shattered the cockpit window.

"Unfortunately it was right at that moment that the vessel hit a small swell and dipped down into the sea. A flying fish, presumably escaping from a predator, flew through the smashed window and lodged itself in the skipper's throat. Shocked by the intrusion and with arms flailing everywhere, the skipper dragged the ships radio onto the deck in a swelter of wires and bits of metal.

"Pulling the fish out of his mouth by its tail, he swiped it around and caught the cook – carrying a tray of hot coffee – under the jaw. She fell backwards. The tray fell forwards, spraying scalding hot drinks over everyone in the vicinity – including the now recovering diver.

"Screaming in agony and clutching his injured eyes, he misjudged his timing and fell over the side of the boat straight onto the head of a surfacing diver.

"With two injured divers, A GPS that showed our position as being somewhere in Mongolia, and no obvious way to summon assistance, I quickly took control of the situation by firing a Very pistol flare to attract the attention of a nearby fishing vessel.

"Unfortunately the incendiary landed right on top of their fuel canister and set fire to the boat. But not before they'd sent off an emergency radio call that summoned several rescue craft to the scene.

"I learned a lot about diving from that," said Krabbmann.

"The main lesson being that losing your marbles and panicking never, ever makes a bad situation better!"

CHAPTER 48
MOCHA DO ABOUT NOTHING

(With apologies to Will Shakespeare who, if franchised coffee shops had been around in his day, would probably have amended one of the lines in 'Macbeth' to say: "Coffee, Sir, is a great provoker of three things: odorous garments, wakefulness and urine.")

Because of its contributing role in the onset of decompression sickness, divers are always warned about the problems of dehydration. It's the reason that they're urged to drink plenty of fluids before and between dives. And not just any old fluid! Ignoring the prejudiced comments of people like W.C. Fields - who, when asked why he didn't drink water replied, "Because fish f**k in it!" - most authorities agree that this most simple of drinks is the ideal diving tipple.

It's a common sense approach to diving health that still manages to escape the attention of some folks. Especially wet-suit clad, cold-water divers who welcome the temporary comfort that hot coffee's diuretic properties bestow on them mid-way through a dive!

Mind you, there's far more to coffee than the kidney-stimulating qualities of caffeine. Even the simple act of having a cup of coffee with friends has, in recent times, achieved a whole new dimension. As I recently discovered when I joined Krabbmann and his friend, Gretta Wrassebender at a kerbside table outside his favourite coffee shop.

"Have either of you noticed how much more complicated diving's become in recent years?" he asked. "It's not that long ago when advancing your diving qualifications was restricted to completing the next training module in a small number of rigidly defined, experience-based courses available at any local dive store.

"And regardless of your certification level and qualifications," he continued, "you weren't faced with a choice of what to put in your cylinder. All that was available was air, air, or air. Nowadays, going diving's not so easy. Even getting a cylinder filled has become a major exercise."

Seeing that his speech was heading down an already well-trodden path, I excused myself by offering to buy the coffees.

"What'll you both have?" I asked.

"I'll have a hot, skinny latte, grande size," said Gretta Wrassebender. "I know the barista here, so tell him that it's for me and he'll scald the milk to the temperature that I like."

"And I'll have a single-shot macchiato", said Krabbmann, "and, if you wouldn't mind, a puppaccino for my dog, Porky. Best make that a Tall for me and a venti for Porky."

I joined a queue of people shuffling slowly towards the ordering station. "A hot, skinny latte, grande size for Gretta over there – apparently she knows a bloke who works here called Barry Star who knows how hot she likes her milk. And I'd also like a tall Porky and a venti puppaccino for the straight macchiato over there, and a venti-sized long black coffee for me, please."

"We don't do Long Blacks in venti." I was told. "You can only have long black in grande! You've got to say, 'grande' if you want a larger long black than a shorter long black, otherwise I won't do it!"

I relented, joined a second queue where I waited for fifteen minutes before receiving the order and returned to the table to hear Krabbmann still complaining about his recent experiences at a local dive store.

"All that I wanted was a nitrox fill," said Krabbmann. "First of all, I was asked to produce a nitrox certification card. Then I was quizzed about what blend I wanted? When the cylinder was filled, they supervised my analysis of the oxygen content; invited me to complete and sign a filling log, and then mark the tank with my name, the date, the oxygen content, and the Maximum Operating Depth of that particular mixture.

"Diving", he continued, "used to be so effortless when ..."

Still smarting over just how much the four coffee's had cost me, I interrupted his flow. "Life in general was much simpler when, if you wanted a hot drink, you could waltz into the nearest 'Greasy Spoon' café, order a coffee poured from the same urn as the tea and lightly garnished with ash from the cigarette that was a permanent fixture in the corner of Doris the Waitress's mouth. Best of all, you'd be back out on the street in twenty-seconds flat with plenty of change left over from a twenty-dollar bill."

"Ah!" Krabbmann said. "But you have to admit that the superior quality of today's coffee is well worth the extra waiting time and cost."

"It's a bit like getting a cylinder filled, isn't it?" I replied. "And just in case it hasn't percolated through to your sock yet, Porky's just treated your shoe with the same contempt that you reserve for dive store professionals concerned about your health and safety! I think he'd have preferred a drink of water!"

CHAPTER 49
THE WONGS OF A DIVE

Everyone who's been privileged to hear me sing – usually after I've had several pints of *Old Cobblers* in the front bar of The Sozzled Cod - claims disbelief when I tell them that, as a young sprog, I was a valued member of the church choir.

Strangely enough they have no problem believing me when I tell them that not only was I briefly in the choir, but that I was once a soloist whose pure rendition of, *"Oh For The Wings Of A Dove"* managed to bring tears to the eyes of an entire congregation. (Indeed, it was such an obviously moving performance that when I started singing the bit about, *"I would fly far away"*, several kind-hearted souls started organising a whip-round to pay for an air-ticket!)

Immediately following my debut as a soloist – and obviously inspired by jealousy of my golden tonsils - the other choristers campaigned to have me removed from their ranks. They claimed that my singing was foul and that my voice, rather than just breaking, had shattered into a thousand irretrievable pieces. I pointed out that a dove is not a fowl and that their decision would leave the world a poorer place by denying it the talents of a gifted vocalist. My pleas fell on tone-deaf ears.

Still determined to make a singing come-back, the likes of which even a peach like Nellie Melba would have been proud of, I spent years banished to the bathroom practicing and rehearsing that ill-fated song, *"Oh For The Wings Of A Dove"*. A self-imposed mission that, with the passing of time, has left me deeply suspicious and resentful of anything that has the word 'dove' in it!

(This includes bathroom toiletries. I've never quite understood why some manufacturers think that their products are more marketable when they're likened to a dove. Soap, I can accept. But I do have problems with toilet tissues. Advertisements that claim, "You'll love the dove-like softness of ..." always make me wonder about the product's quality testing programme and what they do with the doves afterwards.)

But I digress. I know that the dove is supposed to be the symbol of peace and deliverance, but as far as I'm concerned it's just an upper-class pigeon that's tried to better itself by slimming down a bit; a physical condition that's probably due to the fact that it seems to spend all of its time - according to all of the cartoon images that I've seen – flitting around with a heavy olive branch clenched in its beak!

Not once have I ever seen a caricature of a dove feeding on an endangered marine species; nor have I ever heard of a dove doing anything remotely connected with diving, (unless you count those divers who occasionally go, *"Coo!"* when they see a new piece of equipment that they covet.)

Which is why I find it strange to see an increasing number of divers using the word, "dove" to describe their diving experiences.

As far as I can make out, the past tense of diving is, "dived"; as in, "We dived the wreck of the *'Grumpy Grouper'*." An alarming number of people, however, are starting to say, "We dove ...": A term that's only marginally better than, "We doved ..."!

I mention this because of the long-term implications for diving. If 'dove' is allowed to take hold as a commonplace term then it's only a matter of time before **'divers'** will start to be referred to as **'dovers'**.

Apart from the confusion that it'll cause to people living in the southern English seaport of Dover, there's always the possibility that 'dovers' may start to be confused with pigeon-fanciers. And given the measures that most countries now have in place to halt the spread of avian-flu, it's not inconceivable that a conscientious customs officer might ruin an international dive trip before it's even begun by impounding a dover's dive gear and placing it in long-term quarantine.

Not that it's going to affect me. I know the difference between a dive and a dove. Which is more than can be said for those divers who have problems with their vowel movements.

Mind you, I have always wondered why Long John Silver stomps around the deck of a pirate galleon with a carrot called Colly perched on one shoulder?

CHAPTER 50
FIRKIN ABOUT

According to a recent article appearing in *The Bulletin* magazine, international visitor arrivals to Australia have declined significantly in the past year. And that's despite a huge, multi-million dollar international advertising campaign centred around the controversial catch-cry, *"Where The Bloody Hell Are You?"*

For all the good that it did in giving tourism a boost – and bearing in mind the fact that other countries and cultures aren't necessarily in tune with the Australian fondness for colourful idiomatic expressions - the campaign slogan might as well have said, *"Bugger Off Then, You Bastards!"*

Included in that same *Bulletin* article was a quote from a diving industry insider, who stated that dive tourism in Far North Queensland was down by between, "17% to 19%" in the past year; and that, "The last three to four years have been the worst time I can think of in 37 years of business."

Taken at face value it's a disturbing statistic. But it's nothing that a good bit of spin doctoring can't show in a positive light.

Especially now that economics has come out of the academic closet and demonstrated that peaks and troughs are regularly occurring cycles every bit as natural as the changing seasons of the year.

Indeed, when viewed against recent world events and the consequent global slump in tourism numbers, the fact that diving is ***only*** down by 17% to 19% in the past year is pretty good going. Particularly given its meteoric rise in popularity over the previous three or four decades and the mind-boggling increase in the number of people, (variously estimated as being in the tens of millions world wide) who've been introduced to diving during that period.

Mind you, that's no cause for complacency: And as for hoping that the next upswing on the economic roller coaster is close at hand? It may not be! And even if it is, conventional wisdom holds that there's no better time to promote a product - or activity - than during a slowdown in its appeal.

However, as the recent Australian Tourism campaign highlighted, even big dollar advertising budgets don't always produce the desired results. Like the proverbial curate's egg, most mass-media advertising programmes are good in parts, but as the CEO of a major global organization once stated when asked about his billion-dollar advertising budget, *"Only 50% of it works: And if I could determine which 50% it is, I'd cut my costs by half and save an awful lot of money."*

Which leads me to the point of this rant: With little money to spend on meaningful mainstream promotion, (and having, in the past, proven that a broad 'shotgun' approach in trying to lure people away from other water-based activities like boating, surfing and fishing doesn't really work) it's time for dive operators to go back to basics and target fresh new markets.

I've been giving the matter some thought, and it seems to me that the ideal target group is one that already shares a lot in common with diving. Take Morris Dancing, for example!

(For the benefit of those who may not be familiar with Morris Dancing, it originated in the UK about six hundred years ago and has since spread around the world. It's a sort of folk art, in which dance troupes dress up in funny costumes and clogs, tie bells around their ankles and hop and skip about the streets whacking each other with long flat-bladed sticks while chanting things like, *"With a hey nonny, nonny."* After which they all rush off to the nearest pub for a firkin or two of cider.)

The beauty of targeting Morris Dancers is the fact that they're already conditioned to think like divers. Even though it's not a competitive activity, the dance troupes are referred to as teams. And with each team usually consisting of between six and eight dancers, there're enough people to fill a dive course – as well as your average dive boat.

As for training, just like diving you can't walk in off the street and expect to immediately start batting people around the head with a big stick. (Which is probably the reason why Morris Dancers are often seen clutching a white handkerchief in each hand! Mind you, apart from demonstrating the "equipment intensive" aspect of the activity, the use of ***two*** white handkerchiefs also highlights their concern with redundancy – and the fact that they wash their gear after use.)

Best of all, getting Morris Dancers onside and giving diving a leg up won't be an expensive exercise. All it'll take is a firkin or two of cider. Granted, I've no idea how much that's going to cost, but from what I understand about firkin economics, it'll be cheaper and more effective than trying to run a champagne campaign on a beer income!

CHAPTER 51
A FUNNY THING HAPPENED ON THE WAY TO THE FORUM

If Microsoft's founder, Bill Gates, ever finds time to go diving, then I like to think that he appreciates the money that I've invested in software and internet access fees. OK - so his share of my personal contribution may only amount to the cost of one new 'O'-ring each year, (a sum so small that a 'thank-you' letter from him is probably out of the question), but when added together with the fees paid by the hundreds of thousands of other divers around the globe who regularly surf the net, there's certainly sufficient funds to ensure that Bill goes diving in style with nothing but the best in state-of-the-art equipment. He deserves it.

Like many other underwater pioneers, Bill Gates' contribution to diving has largely gone unnoticed and unremarked; an omission that probably hasn't caused him any loss of sleep, but an achievement that, nevertheless, deserves to be acknowledged. Thanks to the widespread introduction of personal computers, user-friendly software programmes and easy access to the internet, going diving has never been easier.

Setting up shop windows along the information superhighway, retail facilities, resorts, live-aboards, equipment manufacturers, training organisations, associations, clubs and diving publications, (like Dive Log) are just a mouse-click away. While some sites are as large and as varied as department stores others - particularly those pages maintained by individual divers - are like market stalls stacked with personal bric-a-brac and fascinating information on marine life, wrecks and exotic dive locations.

Often accompanied by stunning images, the amount of readily available information on all aspects of diving is mind-boggling. With hundreds of thousands of sites to choose from, researching that next dive vacation or equipment purchase is no longer a frustrating and time-consuming chore.

But possibly the Internet's biggest contribution to diving has been the advent of forums and newsgroups. Pick a diving related topic - from underwater photography through to hyperbaric medicine or rebreathers - and the chances are that there's a specialised forum or discussion group that allows people in countries as far apart as Finland and Patagonia to share their views and opinions with other like-minded enthusiasts.

Reduced to words on a computer screen, (and with none of the inhibitions imposed when physically confronting a 250-pound giant who adds emphasis to each of his dogmatic opinions by smacking one clenched fist into the palm of the other while looking you straight in the eye) ideas, information and knowledge pass quickly around the world. And anyone can play! While a doctor in Alaska discusses the pros and cons of in-water recompression with a dive instructor in Phuket, the nurse in Kansas can ask questions about ice diving with a research scientist in Moscow.

Seldom governed by rigid rules of behaviour other than those that might be imposed by the list owners, free flowing conversations develop. What began as a general question about the merit of various brand name fins can quickly drift away into a discussion about which sea-weed to use when making sushi.

While most forums make newcomers welcome some, particularly those dealing with the more esoteric aspects of technical diving, are notorious for the ferocity of their debates and the savage, often uncomfortable and physically impossible responses that follow questions like, "Where should I stick my snorkel when cave diving?"

Others - the cyber-space equivalents of a live-aboard dive trip - are more tolerant, believing that the ability to maintain a conversation coupled with a sense of humour is as important as diving experience.

That few of the thousands of contributors to these diving forums have met, or will ever meet, face to face is unimportant. What matters is that they all share a passion for diving and – through their interest and enthusiasm – help maintain its growth.

It's often said that next to diving itself the next best thing is talking about it. And how they talk! Before I discovered diving discussion forums, night diving was an uncomfortable business that invariably meant getting wet and cold. No longer. Now I can sit back in front of my PC screen, a cup of coffee in one hand, a sea-water spray dispenser in the other, and a fan set at force 4 on the Beaufort scale, (just to add that dash of credibility) while I dive into the world's best locations.

There's no gear to wash or to worry about afterwards - and best of all, Bill Gates provides all of my equipment. Apart from actually getting wet, diving doesn't get much better than that.

CHAPTER 52
THE THINGS WE DO FOR LOVE

According to a statistical survey that I read somewhere or other forty percent of the world's adult population are, at any one time, actively engaged in the search for a suitable partner while another forty percent are anxiously trying to remove themselves from a relationship turned sour.

Not that this has any direct bearing on diving, but as any person who has spent time observing otherwise happy and compatible couples will attest, diving with a soul mate can sometimes put a strain on the strongest of relationships.

Convinced that their affection for one another will grow stronger through a shared experience - and that, *"the couple that plays together stays together"* - they view diving as the perfect activity: And why not? As a recreational pursuit it can be enjoyed on an equal footing by almost everybody regardless of age or gender; it requires only a modest degree of physical fitness; and, best of all, it relies on the buddy system.

Considered in that light, learning to dive sounds a bit like ballroom dancing but without the need to brush your hair or wear sequins.

There's a Yin and a Yang in most close partnerships; a trade off in which the eccentricities of one complements the idiosyncratic behaviour of the other and where each, in turn, becomes either a follower or a leader according to their relevant strength or weakness in any given situation. It's something that can work well on a shopping expedition where one person buys and the other pays, but put those same two people together in the water and even the most harmonious relationship can be stretched to breaking point.

The problems often begin when one PWP (Person With Partner) decides to take up diving and convinces the other that it would be fun if they were to learn to do it together.

(At this point it needs to be stressed that diving's not something that appeals to everybody. While most people can quickly grasp the basic principles and master equipment handling techniques it nevertheless remains an activity that they must *want* to do. It's not something that they should feel obliged to do.)

Invariably, the pair will elect to buddy together during training – something that smart diving Instructors usually try to discourage – and in an unspoken agreement they adopt those everyday roles in which the dominant partner makes decisions for the other; behaviour that establishes a pattern for all of their future diving experiences together.

Instead of diving as a buddy pair, each of whom has equal knowledge and ability, the less enthusiastic of the two builds up a dependency on the other. Allowing their partner to assemble their gear, establish the depth and time parameters of the dive and its purpose, they become a passenger rather than an active participant.

Quite apart from the safety issues and the fact that it's often a case of the ignorant leading the blind, these attitudes also accentuate the couple's differences and can lead to a deterioration in what was a previously happy relationship.

"It's no good getting angry with me. You were the one who assembled my tank and told me that I'd got plenty of air. I thought that something was wrong with my regurgitator thing ..."

"It's called a regulator."

"... regulator then! – when it started to become difficult to breathe. Anyway, you had plenty of air that I could have shared if I'd needed to. It's probably just as well that we were only one metre below the surface."

"But that's only because you refused to go any deeper!"

"I've already told you that I'm not comfortable about doing any of those deep dives straight away. And what would have happened if we had been deeper? I might have drowned!"

"That's only because you weren't paying attention to your gauges."

"I couldn't see the point in both of us checking our gauges. And you were the one who told me that we both had the same amount of air in our tanks just before the dive. You didn't lie to me, did you?"

"Of course I didn't lie to you."

"Then why did I run out of air so quickly? And why – now

that I think about it more – were you trying to get me to go down deeper? You're not a very caring person, are you?"

"Well at least I'm not an unattractive one, like you!"

"What do you mean?"

"When you pushed your face mask up on to your head just then, some mucous from your nose smeared itself over your face."

"I don't like diving with you. In fact I'm not altogether certain that I even like you!"

Although the potential for disaster isn't quite so great when a non-diver meets a diver, falls in love and decides to share their new partner's passion for spending time underwater, the risk still exists. It's especially apparent when the more experienced of the two – perhaps lacking patience and understanding – expects more in the way of knowledge and ability from their partner than they would from a novice stranger.

Or when one says something like, "I learned to dive just to please you and now you're refusing to do something I enjoy! If you really loved me then you'd be only too happy to learn ballroom dancing and wear something frilly!"

It might be narrowing the field a little, but the best hope for divers looking for a long-term meaningful relationship as well as a perfect diving buddy is to restrict the search to those who already know how to dive.

CHAPTER 53
IN LOVE WITH LIFE

Although it had nothing to do with diving, a recent newspaper article about the tragic death of an adventurer immediately grabbed my attention. Not least because the story's headline stated, in part, that he had, *"died doing what he loved"*.

Almost a cliché, one that trips neatly off the tongue and that's intended to give a measure of solace and comfort to the family and friends of the deceased, *"died doing what he loved"* is in danger of becoming a bumper-sticker slogan rather than a meaningful epitaph; especially when key aspects of dive planning are overlooked, or ignored.

The acceptance of risk - regardless of depth or location - is, of course, an integral part of any diving activity. It's only when we fail to minimise those risks by attending to all of the fine details of a planned dive that we put ourselves squarely in harm's way and add to the possibility of becoming yet another *unnecessary* statistic.

The operative word in all of this is, *'unnecessary'*. There will always be occasions when, despite all reasonable precautions, the individual comes to grief because of the unpredictable. But for all of those things that we can control and influence, planning is everything.

The old adage, *'Plan your dive and dive your plan'* is a well-worn saying that seldom receives the attention it deserves. While some divers claim to actively practice the concept, others view it as an impediment to diving spontaneity and enjoyment, or even regard it something that only novice divers need concern themselves with; attitudes that are markedly at odds with common sense.

And it doesn't take much in the way of common sense to see that without a little forethought about what might go wrong in any undertaking - and what safeguards need to be put in place to forestall disaster – there will always be the potential for mishaps.

Consider, for example, the departure from England of the First Fleet and its mission to establish a new penal colony in Australia. It's tempting to think that the British government of the day - having had plenty of experience sending its surplus convicts overseas to grow tobacco in Virginia - just loaded up a few old ships with 1,400-plus prisoners, would-be settlers and military, handed them some cricket bats, meat pies and the recipe for beer and told them to bugger off south in order to establish a claim on Australia before the French got there. But they didn't.

Years of considerable thought and planning went into provisioning those ships with everything that the colonists might need in order to survive the first early years of settlement. Included among the supplies were things like, tools, agricultural implements, flour, seeds, livestock, (including just five rabbits?), 600 gallons of rum, 300 gallons of brandy and 10 sets of handcuffs. Also listed in the inventory was one small cask of raisins and - leaving nothing to chance - 5,440 pairs of knickers!

Without that level of preparation – particularly given the laxative properties of raisins - it's unlikely that the First Fleet settlers would have got much further than the outer reaches of the English Channel before having to turn back and re-supply with underwear.

Although that was planning on the grand scale, the same principles apply before undertaking any sort of dive, regardless of whether it's a shore-dive to 5-metres or a drop onto a wreck at 70-plus metres. And even having covered all of the bases in terms of training, fitness, attitude, equipment and all of the parameters of the dive, the diver should still take time to visualise everything that could go wrong and then – without being obsessive about it, or labelled as having a severe personality defect - take every reasonable precaution to ensure that it doesn't.

The fact is that nobody (it's to be hoped?) actively sets out to die doing something that gives them pleasure: like diving. But if it should happen - and is subsequently shown to have been preventable and caused by a planning oversight - then having news reports state that, *"he died doing something that he loved"*, may not reflect well on the victim's diving abilities or knowledge.

In fact, having given the matter a lot of thought, I like to think that if I have to shuffle-off-this-mortal-coil in an unexpected and sudden fashion, then I'd rather it was doing something like food shopping than while out diving.

Being crushed beneath a runaway shopping trolley overloaded with frozen packets of broccoli in the freezer-section aisle of the local supermarket may not be a dignified ending. But it does have the advantage of being unpredictable. Perhaps more importantly, there's a ready-made headline for the local newspaper, *"he died doing something that he hated."*

Best of all is the fact that there's no adverse impact on diving – an activity that I love – by suggestions that it's unnecessarily dangerous.

CHAPTER 54
TURN YOUR HEAD AND COUGH

I may not have had a lot of practice in self-denial, but I've found it remarkably easy to follow the suggestions of concerned conservationists in saying, *'No to shark fin soup'*. At a personal level it hasn't been much of a sacrifice, but it did leave me feeling warm and fuzzy about my small but positive contribution to the cause of marine protection: Until I started to wonder why it is that all of the other bits and pieces of a shark's anatomy fail to attract similar levels of concern?

Slicing the fins from a living shark before tossing the crippled creature back into the ocean to die is, needless to say, a wasteful act of barbaric cruelty, particularly when the only outcome is a small bowl of rather bland soup. On the other hand, 'harvesting' sharks for commercial purposes - where every useful organ and tissue is put to good use – appears to be perfectly acceptable?

Which probably helps explain why I've never had to fight my way through hordes of placard-waving demonstrators attempting a blockade of the local Fish and Chip shop where 'flake' – a pseudonym for shark – is regularly served up with chips. Neither does there appear to be any concerted outcry or boycott of those shops and stores selling wallets, belts, shoes and other fashion accessories manufactured from shark skin: Or health food shops selling pills, potions and capsules containing shark product; or the pharmacies and chemist shops that stock ointments containing shark cartilage used in the relief and cure of acne, pimples and other skin disorders.

Nor – to the best of my knowledge – does anyone seem interested enough to protest the use of shark liver oil as a principle ingredient in haemorrhoid preparations. All of which leads me to think that the thoughtless needs of a few arseholes plays an even greater role in putting sharks on the endangered species list than simply slurping a bowl or two of shark-fin soup.

Not that there's anything new about trying to protect marine life and safeguard the ocean's resources. As long ago as 1899, King Oscar II of Sweden - concerned over the introduction of trawl netting and its impact on the North Sea herring fisheries - convened a meeting of all of the nations of Europe with industries dependent on fishing. Its purpose was to examine ways of conserving the natural economy of the oceans and halt what, even then, was considered to be an unsustainable plundering of available fish stocks.

A little more than one hundred years later and the world's nations are still unable to agree on a universal protocol to protect dwindling ocean food supplies. In the interim the North Sea herring fisheries have disappeared, along with the traditional North Atlantic cod fishing grounds. Even the Southern Oceans – long considered to be infinite in their ability to provide edible harvests for an expanding world population - are now at risk of over-exploitation.

Sharks may be way down on the totem pole of 'sustainable resources', a buzz word that - like many of the other, *must-do-things-to-save-the-planet* clichés – has most relevance when it doesn't involve personal hardship. Nevertheless, sharks still deserve far more respect than we now give them.

Divers have always had a strong affinity with sharks. Particularly In the early years of recreational diving when it was assumed that all sharks were killers posing a potential threat to anyone who dived. Some, a very few, may have been. Others were not. Not killers, that is.

Johnno recently told me about his early diving experiences with wobbegongs, the seemingly harmless carpet-shark commonly found in Sydney waters. "Divers with little understanding of different shark behaviours would often tweak a wobbegong's tail." He said, "In some instances, the shark would rapidly turn around and latch onto the diver with teeth that, while small, were still sufficient to puncture a wet suit and cause minor injury; particularly embarrassing – and painful – if it happened to be on the crutch.

"We regularly warned people foolish enough to engage in this practice", he said, "to wait for a minute or so, until the wobbegong gave its customary 'cough' – a prelude to getting a better grip – and then to quickly pull the trapped appendage free."

Regrettably, sharks don't have that same luxury of being able to cough and pull themselves free from human attentions. Giving up shark fin soup may help stamp out unnecessarily cruel practices, but it does little to help conserve a creature that, if it became extinct, would take with it other groups of creatures who rely on those same sharks for their own survival.

Like Walt Kelly's comic strip character, Pogo, said in the 1979 Earth Day poster, "We have met the enemy and he is us."

CHAPTER 55
GONE FISSION

Competition can be good. Without it – if Darwin and the other evolutionists are to be believed – we'd probably still be at the amoeba stage in our development and obliged to reproduce by fission rather than the more attractive fusion method.

For a single-celled critter frolicking around in the primeval ooze, the decision to have a quick bit of fission-nooky did away with the need to pretend a headache whenever it felt the amorous urge to split into two identical microscopic blobs. It also eliminated the need to ask the question *"Did the earth move for me?"*

Fortunately for latter-day motel-owners, some of those beasties decided that mixing it up with other like-minded cells was a lot more fun than going solo and playing with themselves: Which is why, several hundred million years later, early humans decided that banding together to hunt creatures larger and more powerful than a single individual had distinct advantages.

Facing competition from other predators for available food supplies, those beings capable of working together as a team had a leading edge over the go-it-alone hunter. It was a strategy that worked. Hence the fact that the woolly mammoth, the sabre-tooth tiger and the dodo - and a whole host of other furry, slimy and scaly things that everybody always claims tastes like chicken when they're cooked – have now become extinct.

All of which serves to highlight the fact that cooperation and teamwork stands a better chance of bringing home the bacon than, (despite its superior size, weight and the ability to give a spear-waving human a bloody good seeing to) going toe-to-toe in a punch-up with a woolly mammoth all on one's lonesome.

Diving is – or should be - a perfect example of the benefits of this sort of cooperative effort. Not because of a need to band together and fight off marauding bands of carnivorous kippers – although it's always useful to have somebody else alongside you to attract attention should a gang of pilchards launch an unprovoked attack – but rather that without somebody standing on the surface and vigorously turning the wheel of an air-pump, early divers wouldn't have got much deeper than half-a-metre before finding it impossible to suck sufficient air down an umbilical hose.

The practical benefits of teamwork are many; especially when facing the hostile nature of a water environment. It's one of the reasons why recreational diving places so much emphasis on the buddy system, a concept that's intended to promote safety rather than stifle the competitive urge to go deeper for longer, or to set new benchmarks in undersea exploration.

Learning to collaborate with others is something that all divers are made aware of at an early stage in their training. It's a principle that they're encouraged to practice and maintain.

Many do. Others, however, pay lip-service to the theory before hopping into the water – and then promptly either forget, or ignore all together, the fact that dive planning is a team effort full of attendant responsibilities. Providing that they exit the water at the same point and roughly the same time as their companions (the "Same Ocean" syndrome) they count the experience as another successful dive.

Sometimes it's because of a misplaced faith in equipment technology and its ability to keep them from harm. In other instances, it's because of a failure to consider all of the possible consequences of their actions and what can go wrong when there's nobody around to lend a helping hand should one be needed.

Quite often, however, it's because of an underlying belief that cumulative experience and training are adequate substitutes for historically proven techniques. Regarding their diving achievements as some sort of merit badge that supersedes common sense and sets them apart from a need to be part of the herd, those "experienced" divers who fall into this category are statistically-proven to be more likely to come to grief in an underwater incident than any other.

Failing to appreciate that under water even the simplest problem can quickly escalate into a life-threatening situation unless help and assistance are immediately available, a few divers' persist in spitting in the face of evolutionary development.

Some even manage to qualify themselves for one of the annual Darwin Awards, presented to, *"those who improve the species by removing themselves from it!"*

It is, I suspect, the sort of recognition that even the most competitive diving 'fissionary' would rather avoid.

CHAPTER 56
POT LUCK

My mate, Krabbmann is one of those divers who swear that they've never been affected by nitrogen narcosis. He's adamant that, regardless of depth, he's always mentally alert and in total control of every aspect of the dive.

Insisting that the reason for this apparent immunity is due to his superior intellect and strength of will – claims that are disputed by those who know him well – Krabbmann is in a minority group.

For us lesser mortals, Inert Gas Narcosis is an insidious condition that gradually becomes more apparent with depth. It's an aspect of diving that's as well understood as, say, decompression sickness (i.e. not at all) but whose influence over diver safety can be even more profound.

Popularised as the "Rapture of the Deep" in scuba diving pioneer Jacques Cousteau's 1953 book, *'The Silent World',* some divers are mistakenly convinced that the experience is always pleasurable; one in, *"which the diver becomes a god. If a passing fish seems to require air, the crazed diver may tear out his air pipe or mouth grip as a sublime gift."*

(At a personal level, I've never felt the need to hand off a regulator to a "passing fish" without first demanding to see their certification card. In fish terms, that probably qualifies me as an "officious bastard" rather than a "god". But I digress ...)

Oblivious to the fact that the unpredictable effects of nitrogen narcosis are the primary reason for the broadly accepted recreational depth limit of 40-metres, *"getting narced"*, has, for some divers, assumed mythological proportions.

Believing that the effects are somewhat similar to spending an evening in the Sozzled Cod pub quaffing pints of 'Old Cobblers' beer, many divers remain convinced that being 'narced' is always an enjoyable experience, one that produces a quick high but without the inevitable hangover. It can be. Then again, it can be something frighteningly different.

Although individual tolerance levels vary enormously, narcosis will – like alcohol - affect different people in different ways. More importantly, it manages to impact on the same person in different ways on different days and at varying depths.

In calm, warm waters with extended visibility the narcotic effect may be limited to nothing more than a pleasant sense of well-being. At the extreme level, it may manifest itself as a feeling of omnipotence; one that over-rides common sense and the planned parameters of the dive.

Conversely, a much shallower night dive in cold water and with limited visibility may require considerable mental effort to counter a mounting feeling of uneasiness that, if uncontrolled, can quickly escalate into full-blown panic.

Faced with this sort of uncertainty, some divers believe that their projected tolerance to narcosis is reflected in the ability to perform seemingly simple tasks at simulated depth in a recompression chamber. Mistakenly convinced that their performance in the 'Pot' is a true measure of their susceptibility, they then undertake dives for which they're ill-prepared.

Failing to gradually work their way down to depth over a short period of time, they'll happily hop into the ocean for a planned deep air dive without giving thought to the fact that it might have been weeks, or even months, since their last descent to such depths.

It's an attitude that's remarkably similar to drink-driving in its potential for disaster, and one of the reasons why there's a growing trend towards use of gas blends other than plain air for deeper diving; or – at the 'shallower' depths of the recreational limits – nitrox.

Nevertheless, there's still no magic gas mix that will completely eliminate the unpredictable effects of narcosis. Which is why the old adage, *"Today's dive starts the night before"* still has relevance as a piece of wisdom suggesting that any dive should always be preceded by adequate sleep and rest ... and an absence of alcohol.

An inevitable aspect of diving that's sometimes referred to as the 'Martini Rule' – i.e. each atmosphere of depth is the equivalent of drinking one large dry martini – narcosis is not to be taken lightly. And while it shouldn't be feared, its potential for harm should certainly be respected.

Cousteau wrote, *"Intellectuals get drunk early and suffer acute attacks on all the senses, which demand hard fighting to overcome. "*

As a person who suffers dreadfully from narcosis, I get enormous comfort from Cousteau's suggestion that I may be an intellectual. (If only I could convince my dive buddies of this fact then they might relent and let me join them on some of those deeper dives?)

ZYMURGY INC.

At the close of the first Tec-Asia Diving Conference – held in Singapore in 1996 – several of the speakers repaired to the Billiard Room bar of Raffles Hotel to enjoy a quiet drink. Inevitably, the conversation drifted towards technical diving and the challenges that its future development posed to equipment manufacturers.

Inspired by the efforts of the bar staff, we decided to launch our own equipment manufacturing company that later became, Zymurgy Inc.; a word that, according to my battered copy of the Oxford English Dictionary, is defined as that, "branch of applied chemistry dealing with science of wine-making, brewing, and distilling." Given that all of the company's founders had, from the perspective of consumers, significant knowledge of all three aspects of that branch of chemistry, 'zymurgy' always struck me as an appropriate name!

David Strike

CHAPTER 57
URANUS – THE WORLD'S FIRST NITROX SNORKEL

Claimed by its designers, an international consortium of diving technologists, to be the world's first enriched air snorkel, 'Uranus" attracted considerable interest among those in the technical diving community invited to the launch preview held during the recent Tec-Asia '96 Conference, in Singapore.

Resembling the 1954, U.S. Divers model snorkel, 'Uranus' features an eighteen-inch [45 cm] black graphite tube with one-inch [2.54 cm] bore; a reservoir well at the lower end, fitted with a non-return purge valve for easy clearing, and a soft, moulded mouthpiece for comfortable grip.

Depending from the reservoir well a manually operated spindle valve activates a membrane adsorbent located in a canister midway along the stem of the snorkel, a device that serves to filter unwanted gases from the mix.

Unlike modern conventional snorkels the top of 'Uranus' curves downwards and is fitted, at its end, with an open sided 'cage' housing the micro-chip sensor device, a ping-pong ball shaped instrument that automatically switches the mix to 21% oxygen on the surface.

Presently available in two models for use with 32% and 36% O2 mixes, the designers of the 'Uranus' snorkel predict that there will be a full spectrum of models compatible with all Enriched Air Mixes up to 50% available by the early part of 1997.

"New techniques require new technologies," said David Strike, Marketing Director and co-designer of 'Uranus', "and we believe that this instrument will revolutionise the way in which many technical divers regard the snorkel."

"The concept of a 'Nitrox' snorkel has sparked the imagination of many in the technical diving community," added Wings Stocks, "and we are already well advanced in our design plans for a model, incorporating a twin-hose mouthpiece, for use with all rebreather models."

The design company, Zymurgy Inc. - with offices located in Australia, the USA, and the U.K. - are believed to be presently involved in negotiations with a number of leading equipment manufacturers keen to negotiate the world-wide marketing rights to this exciting new product.

CHAPTER 58
THE POLLY-GAFF GAS ANALYSER

The inherent problem with gas analysers is their frailty. While primary diving equipment is designed to withstand the rigours of harsh environments the support instrumentation is often less hardy.

During 'normal' no-decompression recreational diving a computer or gauge failure usually means nothing more serious than a controlled ascent back to the surface. But in certain aspects of technical diving such a failure can prove catastrophic.

"This is a matter of particular concern in Closed Circuit Rebreather use where the diver is dependent upon maintaining - regardless of depth - the oxygen content of the breathing gas at a safe partial pressure (PO2)." Says, Zymurgy Inc.'s Technical Specialist.

"Although the subject of fierce debate", he continues, "it is widely accepted, for example, that the absolute limit for breathing pure oxygen for any period of time is the equivalent of 1.6 Bars of pressure - or 6 metres - below which depth a diver on pure O_2 is subject to an increasing risk of oxygen toxicity."

While most Closed Circuit Rebreather divers aim to maintain a PO_2 between 1.1 and 1.4 Bars they place a heavy reliance on sophisticated instrumentation to achieve this constant, in some instances employing multiple redundancy systems in the event of a primary failure.

"While this obsession with safety is justified it does place enormous strains on the resources of most divers, particularly during extended field trips." Observed David Strike, the consortium's International Marketing Director.

Invited to seek an inexpensive solution to the problem, Zymurgy Inc. - the international consortium of diving technologists credited with designing, among other things, the Nitrox Snorkel and the 'Mollusc Fu-2' dive computer - brought their vast expertise to bear.

Drawing on the lessons learned by other industry groups faced with the problem of maintaining life in potentially hostile atmospheres they came to the conclusion that a biological monitoring device was the answer.

Faced with the ever-present risk of drilling into pockets of poisonous gas, coal miners of the last century were in the habit of carrying with them a canary in a cage. With its high metabolic rate the canary would quickly succumb to the effects of changes to the atmosphere and provide the miners with advance warning of impending danger.

Employing state-of-the-art plastics technology, Zymurgy Inc.'s design team have created a small pressure-resistant bell jar with screw-in base plate, 'O'-ring seals and a centrally located, non-return inlet valve to which is attached a small hose that plumbs directly into the counter-lung of all currently available CC Rebreather models. With an adjustable exhaust valve located on the crown, the jar also contains a small wooden swing, and two small containers, one holding bird seed and the other filled with water.

Considerable research went into selecting the appropriate type of bird, the team ultimately deciding on a miniature Australian parrot renowned for its non-stop squawking.

Once the parrot is introduced into the jar and the base securely sealed the whole assembly is clipped to a gimbal mounting on the diver's left shoulder in close proximity to his ear.

Exhaustive tests on the **'Polly-Gaff'** gas analyser showed that while the parrot was exposed to the same breathing mixture as the diver he continued to chatter and squawk, a sound easily carried to the divers ear by virtue of water's greater density.

When, however, the PO_2 falls below 0.5 or rises above 1.4 Bars then the parrot will usually fall from its perch and cease to make any noise at all, an immediate indication that drastic changes have occurred to the oxygen content of the breathing mixture.

Although a few wrinkles still remain to be ironed out it is thought that the **'Polly-Gaff'** will, through its novel use of biological controls, add a new dimension to deep diving research.

CHAPTER 59
THE MOLLUSC FU-2
A REVOLUTIONARY ADVANCE IN DIVE
COMPUTER TECHNOLOGY.

Many divers have come to regard Diving Computers as an essential equipment item. But despite advances in software technology – and the introduction of programmable computers – their functions, like their depth capabilities, remain fairly limited.

Adopting a lateral approach to design, the international consortium of dive technologists, Zymurgy Inc., (the same team who, earlier last year, launched the first Enriched Air Snorkel onto the world diving market), have developed a diving computer with 'across-the-board' applications.

Rugged and capable of operating effectively in water depths of 11,000 metres and beyond, the digitally-powered **'Mollusc Fu-2'** is a fully programmable computer with adaptive features that allow it to be quickly customised to suit each users needs.

. . .

Once the operator has determined which algorithm best meets their requirements - taking into consideration temperature ranges, body weight, age, level of fitness, proposed rate of ascent and descent, maximum depth of water within a 2 km radius of the dive site, intended bottom time, gas mixture(s), and I.Q. - the necessary data is manually entered into the **'Mollusc Fu-2'**, using a unique 'point-and-push' manoeuvre.

Factors determined by pre-dive calculations enable the **'Mollusc Fu-2' to** give a continual reading of gas uptake in nine separate, and individually selected, tissue compartments based on a correlation of time and the deepest point intended for the dive. The off-gassing process can be similarly displayed at any time during ascent by means of the simple data entry process.

A novel feature of the **'Mollusc Fu-2'**, is the low-profile data display. Unlike wrist or console mounted computers that rely on an LED screen, a characteristic that has severe limitations in a silt-out, the **'Mollusc Fu-2'**, provides an automatic tactile read-out of all functions. An attribute that allows it to be located anywhere on the user's body that is within comfortable reach.

"The minimalist approach to design is central to this company's philosophy." Said David Strike, Zymurgy Inc.'s, International Marketing Director. "With the **'Mollusc Fu-2'**, we have created a maintenance-free dive computer that will find equal favour with military, commercial, technical and recreational divers."

. . .

With a full lifetime warranty against mechanical failure and scheduled to come onto the market in early 1997, the versatile, **'Mollusc Fu-2'** is expected to retail for less than the cost of a desk-top calculator.

CHAPTER 60
MISSILE FINS
POWER WHEN YOU NEED IT MOST

Most divers have found themselves in a situation requiring unusual reserves of energy. It may be when swimming into a current; positioning an anchor; assisting a distressed diver, or during a long surface swim back to boat or shore.

Whenever these situations occur the diver will usually experience changes in the breathing pattern. Unless steps are immediately taken to restore breathing equilibrium the partial pressure of carbon dioxide present in the diver's body will increase, resulting in a rapid, shallow breathing rate that in turn can lead to the onset of panic.

Posed with solving this dilemma quickly and inexpensively, Zymurgy Inc.'s design team - the international consortium of diving technologists whose previous achievements include the nitrox snorkel and the **'Mollusc Fu-2'** diving computer - have developed a fin featuring an independent, 'power-on-demand', booster device.

Constructed of heavy thermo-rubber with a stocky, wide angle blade and lateral power vents, the **'Missile Fin'** bears a striking similarity to the classic design of the ScubaPro 'Jet' fin. An open heel model employing an expanding stainless-steel spring and rubber heel pad in place of adjustable straps, the **'Missile Fin'** functions as an ordinary fin - until additional power is required!

The '**Missile Fins**' energy drive is provided by super-charged cartridges of CO_2, (similar in size to those formerly used on BCD's), fastened to the outer edge of each fin, slightly forward of the heel spring assembly. Housed within an elliptical, open-front casing mounted onto the fin, the CO_2 canisters are activated by a unique trigger mechanism. Passing through the upper part of each housing, rip-cords pass up each side of the diver's outer leg and are secured to the upper thighs by adjustable metal clamps.

"Because of the need to discharge both cartridges simultaneously if the diver is to avoid spinning around in circles - a problem that we encountered during early trials with the **'Missile Fin'**," says Wings Stocks, Zymurgy Inc.'s, Senior Design Engineer, "the thigh clamps are joined together by a series of thin, telescopically opening, ball-and-socket rods with a central, downward pointing, lever mounted at crotch level. To activate the device the user simply pulls firmly upwards on the lever. It may sound unnecessarily complicated, but in practice it works extremely well!"

"The additional thrust provided by the booster device is sufficient to propel the diver through the water at a maintained speed of three knots for an average distance (depending on build) of twelve metres." Adds David Strike, Zymurgy Inc.'s international Marketing Director. "However, because of the problems of baro-trauma associated with sudden ascents and descents, we have included a safety over-ride in the **'Missile Fin'**'s features.

"Two miniature hydrostatic sensors are located fore and aft within each unit, devices that only permit operation when the diver's body is angled within 15 degrees either side of the horizontal plane."

Quickly disassembled for easy maintenance and to allow quick cartridge changes, each set of 'Missile' fins comes complete with four spare CO_2 cylinders.

CHAPTER 61
WEIGH-2-GO
WEIGHT FOR THE TRAVELLING DIVER

For those divers who, when travelling, prefer the convenience of using their own equipment, Zymurgy Inc., have developed a range of portable weights that won't put your airline baggage allowance over the top!

The brain-child of Zymurgy Inc.'s Junior Design Engineer, Richard Nicholls, the **'Weigh-2-Go'** series features 1, 2, 3 and 4 kg weights in a variety of mix-'n'-match hues for complete colour co-ordination with the rest of your diving equipment.

Constructed from sturdy polypropylene the 'weights' are hollow containers marginally larger than the 'normal' lead variety and contoured to mould themselves comfortably to the body. Each canister features two low profile, screw-top, filling caps, one allowing ingress of water while the other permits the escape of residual air.

Threaded onto a conventional webbing belt the whole unit is lightweight and easy to carry until required for use. Once at the dive site the user simply fills the containers with the water into which they will dive, either salt- or fresh.

"The beauty of the Zymurgy Inc., **'Weigh-2-Go'** weighting system," said David Strike, International Marketing Director for the consortium of Diving Technologists who constitute the Board of this dynamic R&D company, "is its ability to quickly adapt to any density of water without the need to add or subtract weights from the main component."

"It must be remembered, however", adds Director, Richard Nicholls, "that a 'filled' unit is only completely valid in water conditions approximating, or identical, to that within the container. As an example, fresh water - weighing approximately 3.00 Kpa - is considerably lighter than ocean water that weighs about 3.07 Kpa. Diving with fresh-water filled **'Weigh-2-Go'** units in the ocean will give a normally perfectly weighted diver positive buoyancy. Whereas a diver using salt-water filled **'Weigh-2-Go'** weights in a fresh-water environment will be negatively buoyant."

A minor consideration when viewed against the advantages of carrying your own perfectly weighted system with you whenever you travel.

CHAPTER 62
TITANIC II: A REBREATHER BREAKTHROUGH

Having recently spent an entire weekend at an exhibition surrounded by all that's new and wonderful in diving, I began to appreciate the fact that even if you do build a better mouse-trap, the world is not going to beat a path to your door unless you tell them about it.

Resting on your laurels is not an option when it comes to marketing. Which is probably why Zymurgy Inc. - the Diving Research and Development company that a few of us established ten years ago to market the Nitrox Snorkel – has fallen on hard times.

Determined to not be left behind by developments in diving technology - and once again proving that the only barriers that exist in diving are the self-imposed limitations of logical thought - the Zymurgy Inc. R&D team have developed their own Semi-Closed Circuit Rebreather, the ***'Titanic II'***.

Appreciating that unit cost has been a major factor affecting the widespread introduction of rebreather technology, the design team set out to produce an inexpensive model peculiarly suited to the Australian and New Zealand markets

With minor modifications, but employing a system common to all rebreathers, the '***Titanic II***' features a gas supply, breathing bag (or counterlung), gas-flow regulator, breathing hoses and a scrubber mechanism to remove carbon dioxide from the exhaled gas. "But it's in the choice of materials and the operational mechanics that the '***Titanic II***' differs from other more conventional rebreathers," said Zymurgy Inc's international Marketing Director, David Strike.

Featuring conventional large bore breathing hoses, 3-litre, oxygen enriched air cylinder, gas control and by-pass valves and specially adapted BCD, the '***Titanic II***' employs a chest-mounted counter lung to reduce breathing resistance.

"We gave considerable thought to the selection of a suitable breathing bag," said co-Director, Earnest Krabbmann, "one that was inexpensive, easy to obtain and which lent itself to field maintenance. After considerable testing we finally settled on a 6-litre bladder from a cask wine produced by an obscure West Australian vineyard."

"Quite an acceptable drop, as I recall," added Strike. "Although the hint of strawberry on the middle palate was rather overshadowed by the wine's somewhat astringent qualities."

"During a normal rebreather cycle", Krabbmann continued, "the exhaled gas passes through a chemical scrubber that removes carbon-dioxide. This usually consists of either soda lime pellets or the more expensive lithium hydroxide, neither of which are readily available from your neighbourhood supermarket."

"This fact caused us to consider more revolutionary methods," said Strike. "You could say that we found inspiration in the sea itself. Water can, when in its gaseous form - steam - be used to power the engines of mighty vessels like the '***Titanic***'; the same water which, when in its solid state - ice - can also cause catastrophe. We therefore determined to perfect a cryogenic system that would fill a dual role. One: to keep the drinks cool. Two: to act as an efficient CO_2 scrubber."

During the exhalation cycle of the '***Titanic II***' system, the movement of the gas causes minute fibres embedded along the inner surface of the exhaust hose to vibrate. These vibrations are harnessed to produce electricity that in turn activates a small, but powerful, pump located on the downstream side of the hose's non-return valve.

Driving a compressor that pumps an ultra-refrigerant through a sealed unit of metal coils - in a process not dissimilar to that of the domestic refrigerator - the CO_2 rich exhaust gas passes across the series of narrow bore metal coils into a rigid reservoir canister containing a large block of ice. A denser gas than oxygen the CO_2, on contact with the ice, forms into molecular droplets which gather on the bottom of the canister while the oxygen is allowed to pass through a porous membrane back into the loop.

While early field trials of the, '***Titanic II***', have revealed minor flaws in the unit's operational duration - mainly to do with rapid melting of the ice in tropical waters, and the need to constantly surface and drain the canister - the manufacturers' claim that this will prove nothing more than a minor inconvenience to the intended market of thinking/drinking divers.

"It's tempting to say that the '***Titanic II***' is proving to be an unsinkable success as far as those divers privileged to test dive the prototype unit are concerned," said Strike, "Sadly, however, we are still experiencing minor set-backs in countering the unit's negative buoyancy characteristics. Problems that will, undoubtedly, be resolved before the unit makes it's debut in a liquor store near you sometime before the year 20..."

Manufactured by Amazon.ca
Bolton, ON